THE LIBRARY OF EARLY CIVILIZATIONS
EDITED BY PROFESSOR STUART PIGGOTT

Earliest Civilizations of the Near East

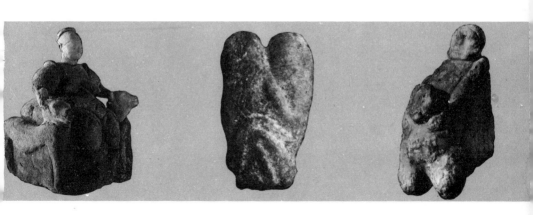

EARLIEST CIVILI

 London

ZATIONS OF THE
NEAR EAST

James Mellaart

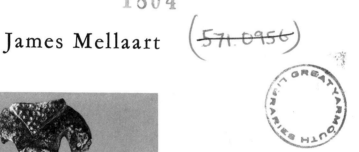

Thames and Hudson

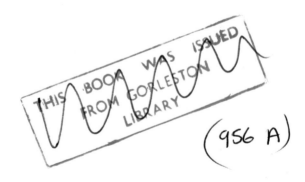

© THAMES AND HUDSON LONDON 1965

PRINTED IN ENGLAND BY JARROLD AND SONS LTD NORWICH

CONTENTS

GENERAL EDITOR'S PREFACE

The circumstances of the origin and early development of agriculture in the Old World have for long, and rightly, been regarded as among the outstanding problems of archaeology. It is now many years ago that Gordon Childe, when making his brilliant pioneering studies in this field, coined the phrase 'The Neolithic Revolution' to denote this stage in man's early mastery of his natural environment, when subsistence-economics shifted from that of the hunter and food gatherer to that of the herdsman and farmer. Childe chose the phrase because of its overtones associating it with the Industrial Revolution of recent European history, when technological innovations, resulting from the development of new forms of power and production, once again acted to modify the entire social systems of peoples.

In the development of prehistory over the past twenty years or so, the problems of early agriculture, and the initiation of settled farming as a way of life, have been to the fore, and it is perhaps here that some of the most remarkable new contributions to our knowledge of antiquity by the techniques of archaeology have been made. It is interesting, in recent retrospect, to realize that the elucidation of the peculiarly complex questions involved could only have been brought about by the development of new techniques in archaeology as a whole during the same period. The necessities were more than those contained within the older archaeological disciplines of stratigraphical excavation, pottery and stone typology, and the rest. The problem involved, after all, more than man and his inanimate artifacts; it was concerned with the animals he hunted, herded or ultimately bred, and with the plants he gathered and finally cultivated. These are of course man's living artifacts – domesticated cattle are as man-made as pottery, and cultivated barley as modified by man as the flint blades and wooden haft of the sickle with which it is reaped. But to examine such problems there had to be an approach by interdisciplinary methods. In these, it was possible to develop a series of closely linked techniques of investigation in which the archaeologists and the appropriate natural scientists co-operated on an equal footing.

Such as approach had been developed over half a century ago in northern Europe, notably in the Scandinavian countries, to deal with just such problems of local prehistory, and from there they were adopted and developed in England in the 1930's. Their employment was the outcome of a particular form of intellectual approach to archaeological problems, in which excavation was seen as a means of extracting the maximum information from sites often not over-rich in more obvious archaeological material, and with a view to reconstructing as much of the total content of the original culture as possible. But the technique of excavation in classical lands and the Near East, the critical areas in the inquiry, had originated from the desire of museums to acquire striking antiquities and where possible works of art: the concept of an excavation as outlined above came late, and even now imperfectly. Few have demonstrated the immense potentialities of the new methods more successfully than Mr Mellaart himself, and this book, with much else that is critical and new, contains the most up-to-date accounts of his remarkable excavations in Anatolia.

With the development of these new techniques and viewpoints, with excavations serving the needs of, and planned by, a team of archaeologists, zoologists, botanists, climatologists and others, there has come the accession of new knowledge that might be expected. But much of this knowledge would be virtually nugatory if it could not be put within some sort of time scale; not only relative so far as can be determined by comparative stratigraphy, but absolute, in terms of years before the present. Here a second great post-war development in archaeological technique could play its part – dating by means of radiocarbon or C-14 determinations.

Mr Mellaart has pointed out in his introduction the limitations as well as the potentialities of the method: above all, we need far more dates from far more samples derived from accurately recorded contexts. But already we are beginning to see a consistent pattern emerging, particularly for the relationship between the Near East and that part of Europe which first adopted agricultural techniques from the seventh millennium BC. Without radiocarbon dates, of which Mr Mellaart has himself obtained a long series from his own excavations, we simply could not put into chronological relationship communities not themselves in that reciprocal contact which expresses itself in modifications of material culture perceptible to the archaeologist.

In this book we see the first beginnings of agriculture from somewhere around 9000 BC, continuing in cultures in which at first pottery, long thought the main criterion of a 'neolithic' culture, was not in fact made, and then before many centuries have elapsed, the first use of metals – copper or lead or gold, cold-worked from the native metal from the sixth millennium BC. The old technological-evolutionary stages of Mesolithic, Neolithic, Chalcolithic and so on are rapidly losing their crisp outlines, but only because we are now able to perceive something which, because it is more muddled and imprecise, is more human.

STUART PIGGOTT

INTRODUCTION

In the five years that have passed since this chapter was written for *The Dawn of Civilization*, archaeological research in the Near East has progressed so much that most of it is now out of date. For the present publication as a monograph, the chapter had to be not only enlarged, but completely rewritten.

Man's emergence as a food-producer and a civilized being has been the subject of much intensive field-work in recent years and many of the new excavations are still in progress and only known through preliminary reports. With political events hindering archaeological work in Iraq, western Iran has become a centre of new activity. Beyond Iran new discoveries in Turkestan have extended our knowledge eastward and many new finds have been made in Syria, Lebanon and Palestine. New excavations in Crete, Greece and Macedonia have added important new information, but perhaps the most spectacular advances have been made in the Anatolian field.

Although many new excavations are in progress, few publications have appeared. The long overdue Amuq volume has been published, but at a prohibitive price, and its contents add little to our knowledge of the early periods with which this chapter is concerned. The important sites of Jericho and Jarmo are still unpublished, and the preliminary reports on these sites offer little that is new. In the past little attention has been paid to environmental studies and the help of natural scientists has only occasionally been invoked. Now some of the wealthiest 'scientific' expeditions are mounted to rectify this omission, but in the resulting process of conflicting theories based on scanty evidence, the aims of archaeology are almost lost sight of. To define the limits of a culture through survey, to select the site with the greatest potentiality, to excavate it, if possible horizontally, and last but not least to publish and interpret the evidence, are still (or should be) the aims of archaeology. No amount of specialist studies can help us if we cannot establish the date of a site, its potentiality cannot be gauged from a few pits or trenches, and a sequence of cultures, arranged typologically, remains suspect as long as it lacks stratigraphical basis.

Radiocarbon dates – or determinations as the sceptics prefer to call them – have been produced for many a site, but rarely in series and although the results are frequently satisfactory there appear to be some startling differences between radiocarbon dates obtained fresh from an excavated site and those taken later, either from old trenches or from samples kept in museums. Possibilities of contamination in the latter cases often lead to younger dates.

The general picture that emerges is one of flux; opinions are sharply divided and the time has not yet come for a solidly founded evaluation of the evidence. Far more material is needed to reconstruct a pattern of the cultural development of the Near East in this important period.

The present volume therefore represents a sort of interim report, based on the results of excavations up to the end of 1963, on reports and publications and on information received from a number of colleagues, to all of whom the present writer is indebted for their help and collaboration in the preparation of this volume.

J.M.

CHAPTER ONE

The Mesolithic Cultures of the Near East
c. 10000–9000 BC

Although very little is known about the conditions prevailing in the Near East at the end of the Late Glacial period, dated to *c*. 10000–9000 BC, it is quite clear that in this warmer zone the climatic changes were much less severe than in Europe. Nevertheless, recent research has established gaps in the occupation of caves in the mountain regions of Kurdistan, Anatolia and the Lebanon and a low density of population between 25000 and 10000 BC. Regional glaciation is also suggested in parts of Anatolia around 10000 BC, but its effects have not yet been traced in the archaeological record.

In Europe the retreat of the glaciers northward brought with them a gradual disappearance of the large herds of herbivorous animals, and Palaeolithic man's food supply was replaced by more scattered, less abundant and more agile animals such as deer, wild boar and numbers of smaller animals.

Men adapted themselves to these new conditions in various ways, evolving cultures that are known as 'Mesolithic'. They were still food-gatherers, making their living by hunting, fishing and collecting fruit, berries, nuts and edible plants. To help in the pursuit of game and fowl the dog was domesticated. The Mesolithic cultures of Western Europe can be traced over a period of at least

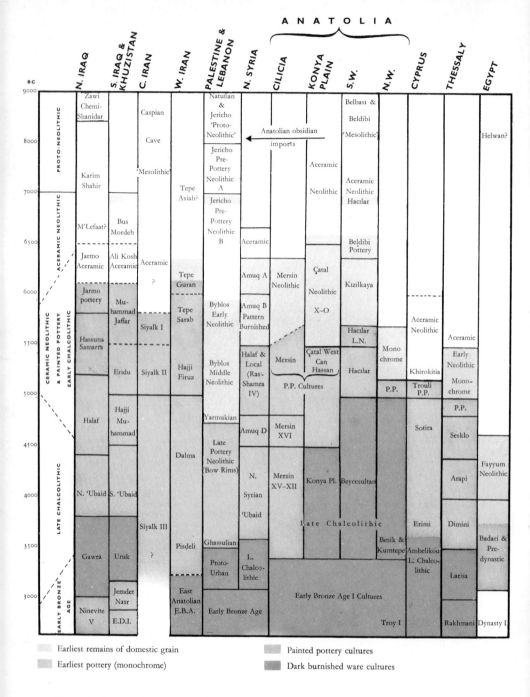

Earliest remains of domestic grain

Earliest pottery (monochrome)

Painted pottery cultures

Dark burnished ware cultures

1 Chronological table

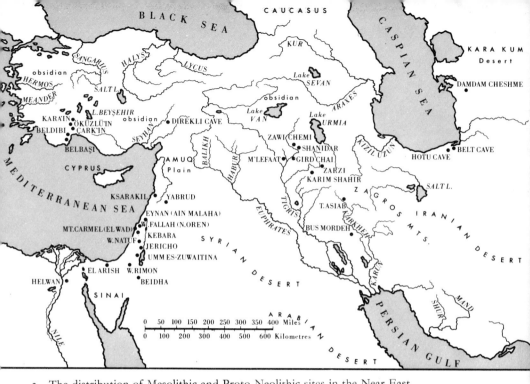

2　The distribution of Mesolithic and Proto-Neolithic sites in the Near East

six thousand years, from *c.* 10000 to 4000 BC, and in many parts even longer. Eventually they were succeeded, in one region after another, by cultures evolving elementary agriculture and the domestication of animals. The two new conceptions of food conservation and production do not appear to have been of European origin, for neither the wild ancestors for sheep and goat and pig, nor those of wheat and barley, had their natural habitat there.

The origins of agriculture and stock-breeding must be sought in the area where these grasses and animals were at home in a wild state, *i.e.* the Near East. Sheep and goat, cattle and pigs had their natural habitat in the well-watered uplands that fringe the Syrian desert or the mountain plateaux of Anatolia and Iran, and the wild ancestors of wheat and barley again are medium altitude grasses, preferring altitudes of 2000–3000 feet above sea-level. Of the two main wheat groups of antiquity, the einkorn ranges in its wild state from the Balkans to west Iran, whereas emmer seems to have been at home in north Mesopotamia, eastern Turkey, and Persia on the one hand, in south Syria, Palestine and Jordan on the other. The distribution of barley again covers the same area from Anatolia to Afghanistan and from Transcaucasia to Arabia. It should be noted that neither these food crops nor sheep and goat are native to Egypt.

Little is known of the climate of this early period, but the presence of denser forests and more open parkland, now reduced by deforestation and overgrazing, implies a slightly higher rainfall. Otherwise the Near East ten thousand years ago is said to have had the same physical aspect as it bears today. Against this background then, so utterly different from that of Europe at the same time, the momentous developments about to take place – the discovery of agriculture and animal domestication – the very foundation of civilization – must now be viewed in the light of the evidence.

The period with which this survey is concerned, extending from the beginning of the Mesolithic, *c*. 10000 BC till the rise of the first literate civilizations of Egypt and Mesopotamia, *c*. 3500 BC – a good six thousand years or more – was prehistoric. No writing existed and we are therefore ignorant not only of what these various peoples called themselves, but also of the languages they spoke. From skeletal evidence, however, some ideas can be formed of what they looked like. All of them were Modern Man (*Homo sapiens*) and at least two distinct races have been distinguished; a graceful Proto-Mediterranean race and a somewhat sturdier Eurafrican race. Both were long-headed.

Ill. 1

This long period can be divided into several phases, the length of which varied from region to region.

Mesolithic, c. 10000–9000 B C (frequently called 'Final Upper Palaeolithic')
Proto-Neolithic, c. 9000–7000 B C (instead of 'Mesolithic')
Neolithic, c. 7000–5600 B C
Early Chalcolithic, c. 5600–5000 B C
Middle Chalcolithic, c. 5000–4000 B C
Late Chalcolithic, c. 4000–3500 B C or later.

The conventional terminology is here used, even though the terms mean little by themselves.

In terms of economy the Mesolithic represents the final phase of intensified food gathering and the Proto-Neolithic the one in which there are indications that the 'Neolithic Revolution' from food-gathering to food producing was well under way. By Neolithic times farming and stock-breeding were well established and in the later phases metal weapons and tools gradually took their place alongside traditional ones made of stone, and the basis was laid for the development of the Early Bronze Age, soon after 3500 B C.

It should perhaps be emphasized that cultural development varied from region to region; some were advanced and others were not. Even today certain communities in the world preserve a palaeolithic or mesolithic economy and essentially neolithic communities exist all around us. In the past it was no different, but nowhere was the contrast between settled farmers and pastoral nomads as strongly developed as in Asia.

Recent research has shown conclusively that civilization did not develop in one specific area in the Near East and spread from there. On the contrary, at least three (and probably more) centres are now known in the Near East; the western slopes and valleys of the Zagros Mountains the hill country of Turkish Mesopotamia and the south Anatolian Plateau.

Towards the end of the Ice Age, some twelve thousand years ago, new groups of people appeared in the Near East, as well as in Central Asia, with an economy which was still based on food gathering. Among the new features introduced were minute flints, called microliths, often of geometric shape, which were evidently set in bone or wooden handles to form composite tools and weapons. Numerous small points indicate that these people used the bow and arrow, a significant technological advance in hunting. From the remains they left in caves and rock shelters, or from open settlements, one can deduce a much more intensified form of food-gathering. Presumably they lived in larger groups and were more organized than their predecessors, but there are no traces of querns and grinding stones, which might indicate the beginnings of a cereal diet. Nor did these people leave any luxury objects, which would have been indicative of leisure and freedom from a constant quest for food.

These Mesolithic groups with their specialized equipment were probably descendants from Upper Palaeolithic hunters, but in only one of these cultures, the Zarzian of the Zagros Mountains, are there some indications that they came from the north, perhaps from the Russian steppes beyond the Caucasus. Although this is far from certain the occasional use of obsidian, a black volcanic glass, indicates relations with the area north and west of Lake Van, where this material is found. The richest site of this culture, Shanidar (layer B2), just south of the Turkish border, has produced a radiocarbon date of *c.* 10000 BC for the culture, and it may have ended around 9000 BC.

Farther east, a similar Mesolithic culture of fishermen and hunters of gazelles was found in the Belt and Hotu caves above the Caspian and in the Djebel cave in western Turkestan.

In Palestine and the Lebanon, another culture, the Kebaran, was at home and a related form, called the Nebekian, was found on the eastern slopes of the Anti-Lebanon, north of Damascus. The tools of these cultures, which are not entirely microlithic, point to an origin different from that of the Zarzian and some parallels are found in yet another Mesolithic culture, that of Belbaşı, on the Mediterranean coast of Anatolia, south-west of Antalya. This latter, however, is much richer in types, including tanged arrowheads and has an individuality of its own. Obsidian was unknown in the Belbaşı and Kebaran cultures, which strongly suggests that they had little or no contact with the Anatolian Plateau. The origins of the Belbaşı culture are of great interest, for it is only in this corner of the Near East that Upper Palaeolithic engravings and mobiliary art have been discovered in the caves of Kara' In, Öküzlü' In and the rock shelter of Beldibi. Moreover, it is possible that the 'Proto-Neolithic' of Beldibi was a development from the Mesolithic of Belbaşı, which would provide a sequence from Upper Palaeolithic to Neolithic elsewhere unknown.

CHAPTER TWO

Proto-Neolithic Cultures   *c.* 9000–7000 BC

Compared to the still somewhat shadowy cultures of the Mesolithic, those of the next, Proto-Neolithic, period are much better known. The new name 'Proto-Neolithic' was chosen to indicate that sometime during these millennia the 'Neolithic Revolution' took place. Although the first domestication of animals is attested, no actual plant remains of this period have as yet been discovered – but this is probably archaeological coincidence – and by 7000 BC we find agriculture well established in Jordan, Iran and Anatolia. Even without actual grain, the presence of numerous querns and mortars, pounders and grinders – which now appear for the first time; the storage pits and the sickle blades all tell the same story of a change in the economy. At the same time we find the first traces of permanent settlements, frequently rebuilt. Cemeteries appear and the graves contain luxury objects such as beads and pendants, which show that man had leisure and time for other things than appeasing his hunger. Art makes its appearance in the form of animal carvings and statuettes of the supreme deity, the Mother Goddess. Trade increases and by the end of the period the first towns are built, already girt with a defensive wall often of massive proportions.

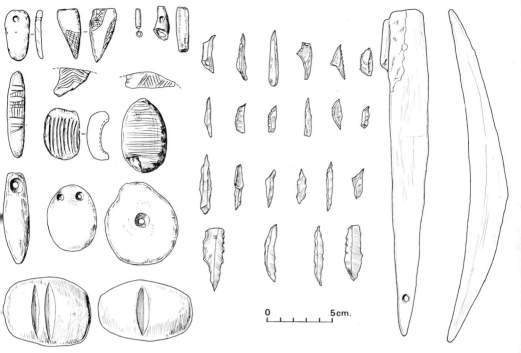

3 Characteristic objects from the Proto-Neolithic of Zawi Chemi village and Shanidar cave. Flint microliths, bone knife with flint blade, sickle handle of bone, grooved stones, incised bonework, stone palettes and beads

The Proto-Neolithic in the Zagros Mountains

The dichotomy of the Near East, already present in the previous period, continues. In the foothills of the Zagros Mountains various cultures follow the Zarzian. In the north Shanidar (layer B1) and the village of Zawi Chemi-Shanidar have produced richer material than the hill-top site of Karim Shahir near Kirkuk. Similar material came from Tepe Asiab in the plain of Kermanshah in Western Iran and the new excavations at Ali Kosh (Deh Luran) in Susiana are full of promise, for they show a deep stratification which was not obtainable on the other sites mentioned. Final reports are not yet available for any of these sites and the following is therefore obtained from preliminary notices.

What started off the transition from Mesolithic to Proto-Neolithic is unknown, but the rise in temperature

Ill. 3
Ill. 4

c. 9000 B C after the end of the Ice Age may have acted as a stimulant to people who were already on their way to more intensified food-gathering. The development at Shanidar from Mesolithic to Proto-Neolithic is considered to have taken place elsewhere, though probably not too far away. Domesticated sheep appear in the bottom level of the settlement of Zawi Chemi (dated to 8900 B C, or 9200 B C with new half life of 5730 years), perhaps occupied only during part of the year, whereas the near-by cave of Shanidar offered better refuge during the inclement winter weather. In the village, oval and circular stone structures were found provided with hearths. These huts or houses had a flimsy superstructure of wattle and daub, or reeds, or matting. Traces of reed matting or baskets were found in the corresponding layer B1 of the cave. Storage pits were found in both cave and settlement and querns, mortars and pounders are a new feature suggesting the grinding of such foodstuffs as acorns, berries, nuts, legumes or cereal grains. Others served to grind ochre. In a grave at Shanidar a flexed burial of a young woman was accompanied by red ochre, a grinding stone and a necklace of small beads. This was not the only grave at Shanidar, for here was found an entire cemetery with twenty-eight burials. Stone walls and arc-shaped settings of stone appear to be connected with a mortuary cult.

The stone industry was well developed; chipped flint celts with polished bits served as carpenters' tools and rough hoes may have been used in early agriculture. Flint blades were set in bone handles; an entire knife with handle from a burial in the Shanidar cave measures eight inches and at Zawi Chemi a little longer sickle handle was found. Sickle blades now occur for the first time, and part of the stone industry is still microlithic, though far less distinct than in the previous period. Trade is indicated by the use of obsidian from the north and bitumen, used

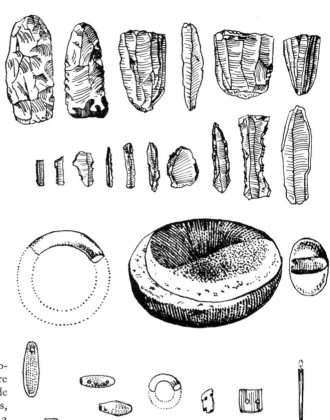

4 Characteristic tools and objects of the Karim Shahir culture in northern Iraq. They include stone rings, beads, bracelets, ground stone querns and a grooved polisher

to fix blades into their handles, came from at least one hundred miles to the south. Particularly interesting are luxury goods; beads and pendants of various stones, such as steatite, greenstone, limestone, marble (?) and even copper; slate pendants with incised designs, stone rings and bracelets (from Karim Shahir), and grooved polishers or arrow-straighteners. Bone beads, rings, awls and pins, perforated animal teeth, a decorated fragment of a palette (?) and some fragments of unbaked clay animal figurines complete the inventory.

Ill. 4

The other sites yielded little additional evidence, Gird Chai produced some obsidian, but like Karim Shahir no buildings. Several superimposed occupation levels – but

21

no traces of buildings were encountered at the site of M'Lefaat, which Braidwood regards as a late phase of his Karim Shahirian culture. There were few traces of hunting here, but likewise no definite evidence for domestication. Finally at Tepe Asiab in the plain of Kermanshah in west Iran, a number of pits were found, one of which contained numerous human coprolites. None of these contained any remains of a vegetable or cereal diet, on the contrary those people appear to have lived on lizards, frogs or toads, perhaps a seasonal diet of semi-nomadic herdsmen, and therefore not representative of the normal economy of the first villagers in the area whose settlements have not yet been discovered.

Our knowledge of this vital period in the Zagros area is therefore still far from complete and much remains to be clarified. Before discussing later developments in the area, we must turn west and describe the Proto-Neolithic Natufian culture, its rough equivalent in Palestine.

The Proto-Neolithic in Palestine and Jordan: the Natufian culture

The Mesolithic Kebaran culture was succeeded by another called the Natufian, which likewise spread all over the country. No genetic links can be established between these two cultures, however, and the origins of the Natufian are not yet clear. The newcomers settled in caves or on the open terraces in front of them in the Carmel or Judaean mountains, or built settlements in the open where natural shelters were not available. Settlement on a natural terrace overlooking marshes and fertile hunting grounds and the proximity of water were naturally favoured; the Carmel caves of El Wad, Wadi Fallah (Nahal Oren) and Kebarah face the marshes of the Mediterranean coast whereas Eynan (Ain Mallaha) overlooks the swamps and pools of Lake Huleh, Jericho owes its origin to a powerful spring and Beidha, near Petra, lay on

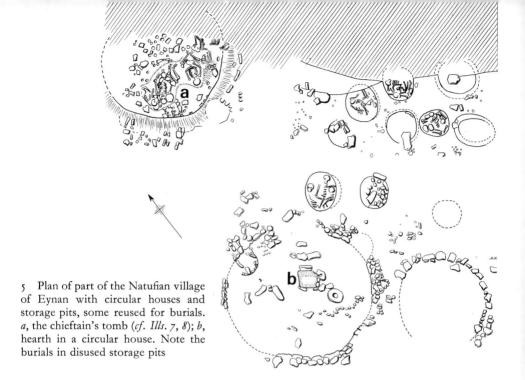

5 Plan of part of the Natufian village of Eynan with circular houses and storage pits, some reused for burials. *a*, the chieftain's tomb (*cf. Ills. 7, 8*); *b*, hearth in a circular house. Note the burials in disused storage pits

a terrace overlooking a wadi. A radiocarbon date of 9551 BC obtained from the possible shrine on virgin soil at Jericho, which is assigned on the basis of some tools to the Early Natufian, suggests that the Natufian culture arrived not much later than about 10000 BC, like its eastern counterpart in the Zagros Mountains. The culture is classified as Proto-Neolithic for good reasons, for although no domestication of animals has yet been established (the Natufian dog has recently been shown to be a Palestinian wolf), sickles and sickle blades, querns and mortars, pounders and pestles strongly suggest the reaping, preparation and consumption of vegetable foods – such as wild wheat and barley, legumes and nuts. Clay-lined storage pits imply the conservation of surplus food, but to this day no actual remains of cereals, legumes or nuts and berries have been found. Moreover, it is clear from the tools and weapons that fishing and hunting still provided the population with the bulk of their food.

Ill. 5
From the important Early Natufian village of Eynan, there is evidence for the following fauna or rather diet: cattle, goat, fallow deer, gazelle, wild boar, hyena, fox, hare, small carnivores and rodents, numerous birds and. fish, tortoises, crustaceans and snails from Lake Huleh. From Mount Carmel we may add bear and leopard, and there is also evidence for red deer, roe deer and horse (or donkey?). From this list sheep, already domesticated at Zawi Chemi is, perhaps significantly, lacking. The fauna from the Early Natufian open settlement of Beidha has not yet been studied, but will probably add ibex to the list.

Fishing appears to have been of great importance to these early Natufians especially at Eynan on Lake Huleh and at Wadi Fallah above the Mediterranean coast. Fish-

Ill. 6
hooks are common finds, but harpoons also occur in the Early Natufian (the only Near Eastern culture which has them), even as far inland as Jericho.

In the cave sites and on the terraces in front of them building remains are fairly primitive. At Wadi Fallah (Nahal Oren) impressive walls hold up the terraces, but elsewhere few architectural features are found.

The discovery of an open-air settlement at Eynan, therefore was of great importance. Three successive permanent villages with numerous floors and alterations, all belonging essentially to the Early (and perhaps part of the Middle Natufian) have been carefully investigated. Each village contained about fifty round houses, with diameters of up to 7 metres arranged around an open central area which contained a large number of plastered bell-shaped pits, probably for the storage of food. The entire village covers at least 2000 square metres.

The houses are built of stone, standing in places to a height of a metre; the floors are partly sunk below ground level, and the stone substructure plastered. The super-structure was probably made of reeds and matting, an

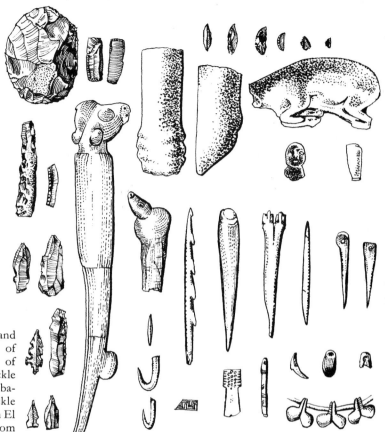

6 Tools, weapons and articles of ornament of the Natufian culture of Palestine. Complete sickle from Mugharet el-Kebarah (*cf. Ill. 9*), sickle handle with fawn from El Wad and ruminant from Umm ez Zuweitina

inexhaustible supply of which existed in the near-by lake. Central posts may have supported a conical roof. Hearths, built of stone, were set roughly in the centre of the room or against the side, and querns and mortars were set in the floors. Frequently child and infant burials were found below a stone slab under the floor. Few gifts accompanied the dead; necklaces of dentalia, a Mediterranean tusk-like shell, were the most common. Some of the finest arrangements of dentalia shells, in diadems or caps came from the contracted burials in the cave of El Wad. Other necklaces were made of the phalanges (toe bones) of gazelles.

At Eynan three different forms of intramural burials have been found: individual burials, collective burials in pits, often with three individuals two of them face to face, and collective secondary burials, *i.e.* the burial of corpses after the soft parts had decayed. The latter often combine fragments of bodies of several individuals in a single grave.

Most of these graves contained red ochre. The most interesting burial of the Natufian culture was a chieftain's burial at Eynan. This belonged to the middle building level and the tomb, possibly originally the chieftain's house, was circular, 5 metres in diameter and 0.8 metres deep. Surrounding the tomb was a plastered red-painted parapet ending in a row of stones with a diameter of 6.5 metres. Two complete skeletons lay in the centre extended on their backs with legs detached after death and bent out of position. One of these skeletons, belonging to an adult male, was partly covered and partly propped up on stones and faced the snowy peaks of Mount Hermon. The second person wore a head-dress of dentalia shells and may have been a woman. Earlier burials had been pushed aside to make room for the new occupants and their skulls were rearranged. Earth was then put over the burials and a stone pavement was laid overall upon which

Ill. 7

Ill. 8

7 Tomb of a Natufian chieftain at Eynan (*cf. Ill. 5*), ninth millennium B C. The tomb, with plastered and red painted parapet covered by a stone pavement with a hearth, may originally have been the chieftain's round house in which he was subsequently buried

8 The·burial of a Natufian chieftain at Eynan (*cf. Ills. 5, 7*). The skeleton was partly covered, partly propped up with stones, facing towards the snowy peak of Mount Hermon, south-west of Damascus

a hearth was erected. Near the hearth was another skull and above this arrangement, covered with earth, another pavement was laid, circular in shape and 2.5 metres in diameter surrounded by a low wall. Three large stones surrounded by smaller ones were set in the centre of the pavement.

This discovery reveals the importance attached to the burial of a Natufian chieftain as well as the antiquity of certain funerary rites which in the pre-pottery cultures of Jericho continued for a further two thousand years. Skeletal evidence shows that the Natufians were physically of Eurafrican stock, fairly robust with long skulls

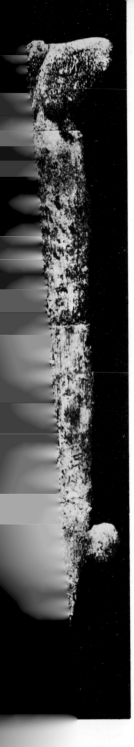

(dolichocephalic). Their average height was a little over five feet.

Something has already been said about the equipment of the Natufians. Their stone industry made exclusive use of local materials and there are no traces of imported obsidian. Flint and chert were used for their tools and weapons; we have rough picks, possibly used for early agriculture, and there are chisels and numerous gravers or burins for woodwork and bone carving respectively. Sickle blades are common and these were set in bone handles, frequently carved (in the Early Natufian) with animal terminals. Microliths occur, but were, *e.g.* at Eynan, not as common as in the caves farther west. Among them lunates, that is, small blades, looking like a new moon, are fairly frequent and these were probably part of composite weapons; microburins for carving are rare. The rich stone industry of Eynan, which is well stratified, is liable to alter the conventional picture of the Natufian as based on previous discoveries. At Eynan, at least, there are no arrowheads, suggesting that the use of the bow and arrow was unknown. For querns and grinders, mortars and pestles local basalt was used, and in contrast to the eastern cultures stone vessels were by no means rare. Basalt beakers were found at Eynan, Kebarah and Wadi Fallah and other fragments of bowls and basins, are occasionally provided with decoration on the exterior. A bowl with dots between horizontal incised lines or rims of basins with crenellated designs in relief demonstrate a desire for ornamentation unattested elsewhere at this period. Then there are pebbles with notches used as fishing-net sinkers, perforated round flat pebbles and grooved stones for polishing bone tools. There are palettes slightly hollowed, still containing traces of red ochre, shells of fresh water mussels, filled with the same material, bone awls for piercing skins, short flat needles or bodkins, bone sickle hafts and flat spoons or spatulae.

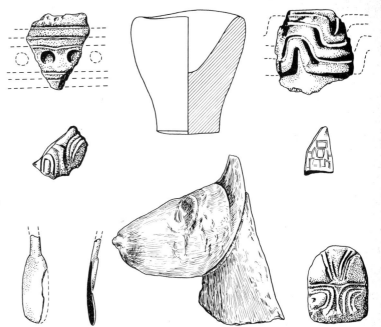

10 Stone carving from the Natufian village of Eynan, a basalt beaker, a schematic human head and parts of decorated vessels. Bone spatula from Eynan and a gazelle's head from the cemetery at Wadi Fallah

And last but not least there is in the Early Natufian a love of art, sometimes naturalistic, sometimes more schematized. The crouching limestone figurine from the cave of Umm ez Zuweitina, or the handle of a sickle from El Wad showing a fawn are superb examples of naturalistic art, worthy of Upper Palaeolithic France. The animal head on the sickle from Kebarah and the recently discovered human heads from Eynan or the gazelle's head from the cemetery at Wadi Fallah show a definite schematization of animal or human portraiture which, however, is most vivid. Nor should one forget the erotic group from Ain Sakhri, now in the British Museum.

Ill. 6

Ill. 9
Ills. 10,
12, 13

Ill. 11

No such works of art are found after the Early Natufian period and it would appear that – like so many of its successors – the Natufian culture stagnated in Palestine. The Early Natufian culture was followed by two later phases (Middle and Late) about which much less is known. The site of Eynan was deserted and 2 metres of

11–13 Natufian sculpture in stone of the ninth millennium BC, the earliest sculpture in the Near East. The two schematic stone heads are from Eynan (*cf. Ill. 10*) and the embracing couple (left) is from Ain Sakhri

14 Early Natufian shrine on virgin soil at Jericho. The round hollows in the rough-plastered floor probably served as storage pits and the querns are evidence for the preparation, if not the cultivation, of cereals at this early date, *c.* ninth millennium B C

sterile sand covers the Early Natufian of Beidha. The later Natufian phases are best illustrated by the cave sites, but the material is almost exclusively confined to stone and bone tools, which are now made with much less care. Arrowheads, frequently notched, make their appearance in the Late Natufian.

It would appear that the real development of this culture was not made in the cave sites, but in the Jordan valley. At Jericho, the Early Neolithic shrine was burnt and a settlement rose above it forming a mound (or *tell*) some 4 metres high. No clear house-plans could be discerned in this Proto-Neolithic village and lumps of clay

Ill. 14

were used for walls. The stone industry is of Natufian type, but obsidian now makes its first appearance, which shows that contact was established with Anatolia. Obsidian deposits are unknown in Syria, Palestine, Jordan, Iraq or Cyprus. The date of this village might fall in the ninth millennium. There are still no traces of domestication of animals or the growing of grain, but the beginnings of agriculture may be assumed to have been introduced in view of Jericho's explosive expansion in the next stage during the eighth millennium BC, which is known as Pre-Pottery Neolithic A.

Pre-Pottery Neolithic A Jericho

The causes of the spectacular development of Jericho from a small Proto-Neolithic village with flimsy huts or shelters into a town occupying not less than ten acres are still unknown to us. There is no break in the Natufian tradition between the underlying 'nucleus tell' and the new town, which may have been built around 8000 BC. The stone industry is essentially a development of the Natufian tradition of the previous phase and now a rich bone industry is added to it.

The explosive development witnessed at Jericho almost certainly presupposes the introduction into this oasis 200 metres below sea-level of cultivation techniques of wheat and barley. It suggests that by now agriculture and not just collecting of cereal food is an established fact. Storage rooms for grain have indeed been found, but from the published reports it is uncertain whether carbonized grain deposits or the impressions of grain in brick and plaster were found. For the domestication of animals there is still no evidence, and the hunting of gazelles may have supplied the inhabitants of Jericho with their meat.

The new town consisted of round houses built of mud-brick (of hog-backed shape) on stone foundations, a definite advance on the flimsy huts of the previous period. Their floors were well below the level of the ground outside and the houses were entered through a door with wooden jambs and down several steps. Most of the houses consisted of a single circular or oval room, 4 to 5 metres in diameter, domed with wattle and daub and the walls and floor covered with mud plaster. Some more ambitious structures had as many as three rooms. The town was not fortified from the beginning and at least three phases of round houses preceded the first erection of fortifications. As the wealth of the settlement grew and powerful neighbours established themselves, city walls became a necessity to protect the town. The defences put up are astounding for any period; a rock-cut ditch, 8.5 metres wide and 2.10 metres deep, cut without the help of picks and hoes. Within the rock-cut ditch a stone wall was built, 1.64 metres thick and preserved to a height of 3.94 metres. Originally freestanding it was rebuilt as the accumulation of building rubbish inside rose and the later two rebuildings give it a height of over 5 metres, which was crowned with a mud-brick super-structure of unknown height. Within the area of excavation a great stone circular tower was found, still standing to a height of 8.15 metres, with a well built inner staircase giving access to the top. Twenty-eight stone steps made of single slabs of stone over a metre wide form the staircase and the roof slopes obliquely. At the bottom of the steps a passage, 3.94 metres long, leads to a door, 1.70 metres high, at the eastern end of the tower. A water channel from the top of the tower drains into a series of well-plastered curvilinear enclosures built up against its north side. A similar enclosure against the south side is said to have been used for the storage of grain. The tower was in use for a long time and two further coats of masonry were added to it at the time of the rebuilding of the city wall and the water tanks were also rebuilt. Finally

Ill. 17

Ills. 15, 16

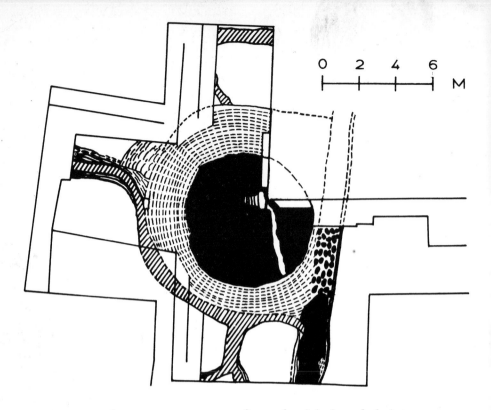

the tower went out of use; burials invaded the passage, the door was blocked and round houses invaded the space of the storage chambers. Again there were frequent rebuildings and from one of them, destroyed by fire, a radiocarbon date of 6935 BC was obtained. Four more levels of round houses follow this date after which the town wall collapsed and denudation set in. It looks as if the town was then finally deserted.

The long life of the Pre-Pottery A town is demonstrated in other trenches and not less than twenty-two phases of building could be distinguished. It is likely that the tower was built soon after the beginning of the eighth millennium.

One question must be raised which has not been answered by the excavations. May we assume that there were other towers like the one excavated at more or less regular intervals along the wall or is this tower the 'keep' or 'donjon' of the settlement serving as a lookout tower

15–17 Jericho Pre-Pottery A Neolithic period defences. Plan of the tower (opposite) and a view of the tower (below) showing the entrance at the bottom. Right, a view of the main trench with the round tower in the background and superimposed city walls, virgin soil and rock-cut ditch in the foreground

like the towers in the *nuraghe* settlements in Sardinia, or the *brochs* of Scotland which are likewise set within the walls? The prodigious labour involved in the erection of these defences implies an ample labour force, a central authority to plan, organize and direct the work and an economical surplus to pay for it. The population of this urban centre has been estimated at about two thousand, which is probably too little. The defences are thought to have been built against the people who finally took over the site in Pre-Pottery Neolithic B, and there is evidence that they were already in Palestine at this period. Evidently their appearance was a threat to the town of Jericho, for no one builds walls this size against marauding bedouin.

One important problem remains to be solved. From what form of economy did Jericho derive its wealth? Wealth is implied by the fortifications, even if little evidence was forthcoming from the deserted town itself. Trade in stock is the first thing to be removed when people leave a place. Hunting and fishing are evidently not the basis for the growth of Jericho and to feed a community of two thousand people or more agriculture must have been practised. It is, however, most unlikely that agriculture should have flourished more at Jericho, 200 metres below sea-level than elsewhere in Palestine. Some other source of revenue must have existed, and this was probably trade. Jericho was well situated for commercial enterprise; it commanded the resources of the Dead Sea, salt, bitumen and sulphur, all useful products in early societies. Obsidian, nephrite and other greenstones from Anatolia, turquoise matrix from Sinai and cowries from the Red Sea have been found in the remains of the town, only a fraction of which was excavated. Had the workshops or warehouses been discovered, many other materials might have been added. In fact very little material of this period from Jericho has yet been published. The stone industry is a development of the Proto-Neolithic and arrowheads are rare. Fine stone bowls have not been found, and containers were probably still made of basketry, leather or bitumen. Burial habits continue without much change; and the dead are buried below the floor. Groups of skulls without skeletons suggest secondary burial and a group of baby skulls found under a basin-like structure may be the remains of human sacrifice.

Jericho is no longer the only site in Palestine of this period. At Wadi Fallah (Nahal Oren) on Mount Carmel above the Natufian layers stone round houses with diameters varying between 2 and 5 metres were found each with a central stone-lined fireplace. The building tradition derives from Ain Mallaha, but the stone industry is different, and has been called 'Tahunian'. Stone bowls (mainly in limestone), polishing stones, elongated mortars, grooved stones, sickle blades, arrowheads, saws, flaked stone axes, tranchets and picks suggest a mixed economy in slightly wooded country. A similar industry has been found at Abu Suwan near Jerash.

Ill. 18

More remarkable is the settlement at Beidha near Petra, two hundred miles south of Jericho. Here the fourth village, occupying about 1.5 to 2 acres consists of numerous partly subterranean houses of sub-rectangular plan, *i.e.* more or less straight-sided with rounded corners. The lower parts of the buildings are made of stone, carefully built in slabs and walls and floors are covered with lime plaster. Each house stands by itself and has kitchens and storerooms attached. The planning is reminiscent of Pre-Pottery A Jericho, but the plaster floors and the 'Tahunian' stone industry with arrowheads and borers, link it to Pre-Pottery B. Seven different stages of building have so far been distinguished; from the fourth from the top, destroyed by fire a radiocarbon date was obtained of 7090 BC with higher half life. The village was then

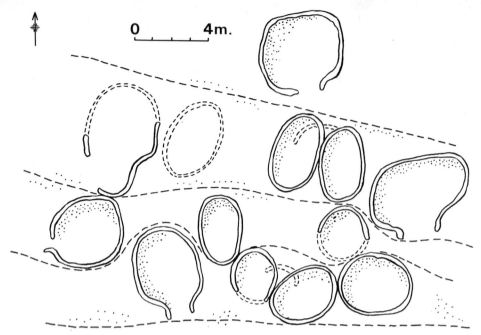

18 Plan of the Pre-Pottery Neolithic A settlement at Wadi Fallah (Nahal Oren, stratum II) with round houses and terraces

probably in use between *c*. 7200 and 7000 BC or there-abouts. Two features are outstanding; the use of coloured plaster, cream, buff, brown and red, and the undoubted presence of numerous grain impressions in the plaster, suggesting that agriculture was in full swing.

As far as we can see, these developments mark the height of a native Natufian tradition in Palestine. The following cultures, the Pre-Pottery B of the seventh millennium are of a northern, Syrian or even Anatolian origin and from then onwards, Palestine, poor in re-sources, seems to have become a provincial region com-pared to the north. The early developments in Palestine may be the result of the natural occurrence of wild wheat and barley in that country. Its absence in Syria may have retarded a similar development there until later times.

CHAPTER THREE

Syria and Palestine in the Seventh Millennium

The Pre-Pottery B culture of Jericho

Around the beginning of the seventh millennium BC a
new culture, which still did not know the use of pottery
spread from the north into the Jordan valley. It is best
known from Jericho, where the new settlers introduced
it on the deserted site, but it has since been recognized
throughout the Jordan valley (at Tell Sheikh Ali I and Tell
Munhatta); the uplands on either side (Tell Far'ah and
Wadi Shu'aib) and it also reached Beidha (third to first
village). The arrival of this culture is marked by a complete break with the old Natufian tradition. The distribution of the new settlements shows clearly that the newcomers come from the north via the Jordan valley. The
tradition of rectangular rooms with plaster floors can be
traced to Ras Shamra (VA) on the north Syrian coast and
beyond to the Anatolian Plateau. Surface finds in the
region north and west of Damascus and recent excavations at Tell Ramad (Qatana) south-west of Damascus
show a similar element established in this region, but
these people have not yet been recognized either in
Lebanon or on the Palestinian coastal plain.

As far as can be seen they did not introduce a change in
the economy which remained one based on agriculture

(the details are unknown), domestication of animals (goat dog and cat? at Jericho) supplemented by hunting, gazelle at Jericho, ibex, gazelle, birds (partridges?) at Beidha. The details are meagre, mainly for lack of study. In the stone industry, small and large arrowheads, mostly tanged and some with beautiful barbs, others pressure flaked, are as typical as long straight sickle blades. Borers are particularly common, but scrapers remain rare. The industry is the 'Tahunian' and flint, plentiful in Palestine and Jordan is the most common material used. Obsidian, however, still appears at Jericho.

Ill. 24

The appearance of long oval querns, open on one narrow side is new; as is also the first appearance of fine limestone bowls and plates, for pottery was still unknown. Baskets, no doubt treated with lime or bitumen to make them impervious, and skins were probably in use but have left no tell-tale remains. Matting, however, is well attested at Jericho, but what is surprising is that people should have made round coiled mats to put in rectangular rooms. This somehow suggests a relic from the earlier tradition, when houses were round.

At Jericho we have good evidence for the architecture of the period. The new settlement appears to have been even larger than its predecessor and was, as far as can be ascertained, only provided with defences in the form of walls built of enormous blocks of stone, towards the middle of the period. The period was evidently a long one; in places not less than twenty-six plaster floors were found one above the other. Houses were constructed of long cigar-shaped bricks, bearing on their upper surface rows of finger impressions, which helped to hold the mortar between the bricks. Stone foundations are common and floors and walls were carefully plastered. The burnished lime-plaster was frequently painted red, but it is unknown how far the red paint was carried up the wall. We may perhaps assume that it formed a dado, about a

19–20 Small shrine from Pre-Pottery B Jericho in a room with red plaster with a niche at the far end containing a roughly shaped stone pillar. Below right, plan of a shrine, the fullest building plan available, rather like the later 'megaron' style of building

metre high. Above that the walls were probably cream in colour, if only not to make the rooms too dark. In one instance there were traces of painting forming a tree or herring-bone pattern on a floor. Not all floors were painted red, there are others in pale pinks, creams or whites. Hearths were neat rectangular basins, sunk in the floor and lined with plaster. Doorways were wide and frequently double and the door jambs were rounded. Ovens and hearths were found in courtyards, through which all communication took place in lieu of streets. What the city plan was like is unfortunately unknown. Several buildings are designated as shrines; the simplest consisted of a small room with a niche at the back, in which a stone stela may have been deposited; another, the fullest plan of a building available, looked like a 'megaron' and may have had columns leading from a courtyard into the building, and a third with a huge room, at least 6 by 4 metres, and curvilinear annexes along the long sides, may also have served cult purposes.

Besides small clay figurines depicting the Mother Goddess or those of animals, associated all over the Near East with a fertility cult, we are fortunate in having at Jericho the remains of larger statuary, which must have represented the cult statues of a shrine. In 1935 John Garstang found the fragmentary remains of two groups of statues, modelled naturalistically in clay on canes or bundles of reeds and painted red. They were thought by him to represent two groups, each consisting of a female, male and child. They were nearly life size, but unfortunately only one head has been illustrated. Kathleen Kenyon found the plaster head and bust of another near life-size figure, but much more schematized. On the other hand, she found not less than ten human skulls, with features admirably modelled in plaster and cowries inserted to replace the eyes. Several of these skulls, which were probably used in an ancestor cult, had traces of painting to indicate the hair and in one case a moustache. They gave one a vivid impression of what the inhabitants of Jericho of those days looked like. The physical type is more developed and finer than the typical Natufians of the previous phase and is known as 'Proto-Mediterranean'. In the upper levels of the settlement a new type of extended burial frequently without the head was found, contrasting with the earlier crouched burial, which, however, does not entirely disappear. At Beidha, crouched burials without heads were encountered, the heads having been removed for some cult purpose, and similar practises are known at a comparable date from Hacılar and Çatal Hüyük in Anatolia.

21 Human skull with the facial features modelled in plaster, the eyes are inserted cowrie shells. Pre-Pottery Neolithic B period, Jericho

Ill. 22

Beidha is a good example of a village of this period and here it was possible to excavate the greater part of the settlement even if at least a third has been swept away by the wadi. Comparatively little survived of the topmost village, but the remains of the second and third are well preserved. In each case heavy stone walls surrounded the settlement which consisted of numerous workshops arranged around one or more residential rooms. Courtyards and passages separated the latter from the workshops which were packed close together and entered from narrow lanes. Some of the main rooms measured 9 by 6 metres and were provided with a circular raised hearth with a diameter of about a metre next to which was a wide seat against the south wall. Floor and walls were covered with several layers of fine lime-plaster, painted with a red dado and band along the walls leaving the centre plain and cream coloured. Later layers were of plain cream plaster. The great size of these rooms in the

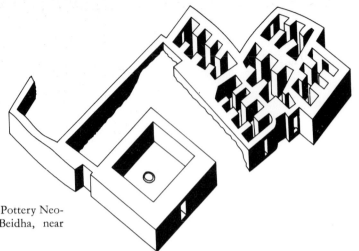

22 Plan of part of a Pre-Pottery Neolithic B settlement at Beidha, near
Petra

Ill. 23

second and third villages first led to their interpretation as
courts, but they may easily have been provided with a roof
of light construction. The workshops have an oblong
plan and are entered through an ante-room or vestibule at
the short side. This leads into a corridor a metre wide
which has three cubicles, each a metre wide and up to
2 metres long, on either side. Separating the cubicles
are wide buttresses which probably supported an upper
storey. One of these narrow rooms was a butcher's shop,
another served a maker of bone tools, a third a bead-
maker and so on. In each case the tools of the trade as well
as finished products and raw materials were found *in situ*.
The considerable number of these workshops creates the
impression of great industrial and commercial activity.
Beidha was probably the bazaar of the district and a remote
forerunner of Petra, controlling the same trade routes
from the desert to the Mediterranean coast at Gaza and
from the Red Sea to the Jordan valley and Jericho. Red
Sea cowries and mother-of-pearl are common, haematite
and malachite both found in the region were collected,
flint was abundant locally but little obsidian seems to
have reached this southern outpost. Limestone was
brought from the hills, calcite collected from the Nubian
sandstone and worked into beads and pendants. Large

23 A bone tool workshop with ibex horns and stone tools in the background at Beidha

numbers of querns, mortars, pounders and pestles imply agriculture, already established in the previous period, but supplemented by the hunt. Small cages found along a courtyard suggest that decoy birds (partridges) were kept, since they are too small to have served as kennels.

Ill. 24

The new radiocarbon dates for the Pre-Pottery B period at Jericho; 6968 and 6918 BC show that there was no long gap between the desertion of the old town and the re-occupation by the newcomers. Even if the earlier C-14 dates of 6250 and 5850 BC are now superseded it is evident that the period (with its twenty-six floors at Jericho) lasted throughout the seventh millennium and perhaps well into the sixth. The end of the culture is obscure; Beidha was deserted and a stratigraphical lacuna separates the end of Pre-Pottery B and the totally different culture of Pottery Neolithic A at Jericho.

Nowhere in Palestine has any continuity been established yet between the aceramic and the ceramic neolithic periods, but evidence is accumulating to show such a continuity in Syria and the Lebanon.

Syria and Lebanon before the introduction of pottery

Ill. 26

Far more research is needed in Syria and the Lebanon before one can hope to present a picture of cultural development parallel to that of Palestine from the Natufian to the first arrival of the pottery-using cultures. There are, however, some surface finds, happily supplemented by a few soundings in the Amuq, at Ras Shamra, Tell Ramad and Yabrud to sketch a tentative outline.

A form of Natufian is known from Yabrud in the Anti-Lebanon and a number of surface sites. The so-called Tahunian industry extends from Palestine northwards over the Lebanon and the Damascus Basin and would seem to have been at home in this region, extending from there southward during the Jericho Pre-Pottery A phase, and culminating in the next. The rectangular houses with plaster floors and the fine stone bowls are also northern features and are known from pre-pottery levels at Ras Shamra (VA) on the north Syrian coast, and from the later Pottery Neolithic of Byblos. This continuity in architecture is noteworthy and is supported by a study of the stone industry. Elsewhere in the Lebanon a neolithic stone industry with very large tools and weapons, 'gigantoliths', occurs at numerous sites (Kara'un culture, Mukhtara, Adlun, etc.) not associated with pottery, and possibly earlier than the Pottery Neolithic of Byblos. Aceramic cultures have not yet been found in excavations, but they must have existed here as is clear from Ras Shamra and from the fact that the Pre-Pottery B complex of Palestine originated in this area, just as the following Pottery Neolithic cultures can be traced back to the

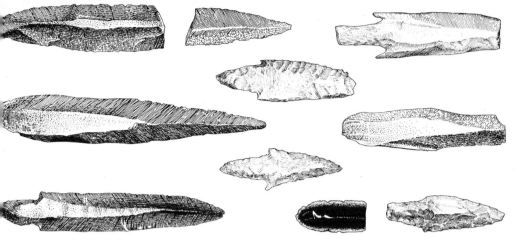

24 Flint and obsidian arrowheads and sickle blades from the Pre-Pottery Neolithic B Jericho industry known as 'Tahunian'

Lebanon. Before we sketch the subsequent developments in Palestine and Syria, the first neolithic cultures of the Zagros zone must claim our attention.

Jarmo

Qal'at Jarmo is the name of a village site, covering about three to four acres, situated on the edge of a deep wadi in the plain of Chemchemal in Iraqi Kurdistan. Some sixteen superimposed floor levels have been established of which the top five are characterized by the first appearance of already developed pottery. The lower eleven are pre-ceramic and stone bowls, baskets lined with bitumen and probably skins served as containers. As villages go it was small and it contained probably no more than 20 to 25 houses with an estimated population of about 150 souls.

Houses were built of clay (locally called *tauf*), for bricks were still unknown and only in the upper building levels were stone foundations found. The walls were plastered with fine mud and a similar cover was spread over a reed matting to make soft floors; later houses were provided with ovens and chimneys. The rooms were small, 1.5 to 2 metres in length but several were found in each house. Sunk clay-lined basins were used as hearths

25 Characteristic objects of the Jarmo Pre-Pottery Neolithic culture. Below left, earliest pottery from the upper levels

26   The distribution of Aceramic and Ceramic Neolithic cultures in the Near East

and pot-boilers were found in several of them. The roofs were made of reeds with a thick clay covering. The dead were evidently buried outside the settlement and human remains are therefore scarce. The economy of the Jarmo settlement is important; for the first time in Iraq agriculture can now be demonstrated. Emmer wheat, morphologically close to the wild form, was present and already accompanied by einkorn wheat and two-row barley, similarly close to the wild form. Field peas, lentils, blue vetchling were grown and pistachios and acorns eaten for their fat. Among the animals only the goat and perhaps the dog were domesticated and pig, sheep, gazelle and wild cattle were hunted. Snails occur in such quantity that they must have been eaten.

The chipped stone industry, mainly in flint but with a substantial addition of imported east Anatolian obsidian consisted mainly of blades for composite tools, such as knives and sickles, the blades being fixed with bitumen into a wooden handle. Microliths, such as diagonal ended bladelets, trapezoids, triangles, crescents, side-blow flakes and scrapers were still common, many being made of obsidian. Some of these points may have been used as arrowheads for hunting. The ground-stone industry was highly developed; apart from axes with polished cutting edges, saddle querns and grinders, mortars and pounders, door pivots and stone balls, there were fine palettes used for the grinding of ochre, spoons, mace-heads, perforated discs and a fine set of marble or alabaster rings and bracelets, many bearing incised or grooved ornament.

The finest stonework, however, is shown in the elegant cups and bowls for which veined stones were carefully selected. Bone was used for awls, spatulae, rings, beads and pendants. Numerous figures of animals and crude figures of the Mother Goddess were fashioned in unbaked clay. Many of these latter are very schematic; small clay balls and cones may have been used as childrens' toys.

Tepe Guran, Tepe Sarab, Tell Shimshara and the date of Jarmo

The appearance of pottery in the upper three layers may eventually help in establishing the chronology of the site. In the top three layers an unpainted straw-tempered ware with jars and bowls with vertical lugs appears in quantity and is probably locally made. This ware is also found at Ali Agha and in the very bottom layers of Hassuna (Ia) and Matarrah, where it is dated to 5790 BC. Below it (in levels 4 and 5) and therefore earlier than 5800 BC, a much finer red slipped or painted and burnished ware 'Jarmo

27 Earliest painted pottery from level 5 at Tepe Guran in Luristan. The scale is in centimetres

painted ware' is found, which was evidently introduced from farther east or south-east. It now occurs in greater quantities at Tepe Guran, south of Kermanshah. The technical quality of this pottery is such that it evidently cannot be considered as the earliest pottery in the Zagros area and an unpainted grey or buff archaic ware preceded it at the latter site. Only the three lowest levels of Tepe Guran were pre-ceramic. The 'Jarmo painted ware' is there succeeded by a finer product, already known from Tepe Sarab near Kermanshah. The Tepe Sarab culture is typologically later than that of Aceramic Jarmo and its pottery, red slipped and burnished or red painted as well as its figurines are far more advanced. The clay animal figurines are remarkably lively, but the same strangely stylized 'foot shaped' figurines appear here as at Jarmo. Fine stone bowls accompany the pottery as at Tepe Guran. Three dates for the Sarab culture have been obtained: 6245, 5923 and 5883 BC. The date of Jarmo itself is, in spite of twelve radiocarbon determinations, far from settled. The excavator prefers a general date of *c.* 6750 BC, but would not allow more than four hundred years for the entire duration of the settlement.

Ill. 27

Ill. 28

More work is needed to prove or disprove a date of 6750 BC for Jarmo, as compared to 5800 for the beginning of Hassuna. What has been established is that independant Iranian centres of early pottery traditions evolved

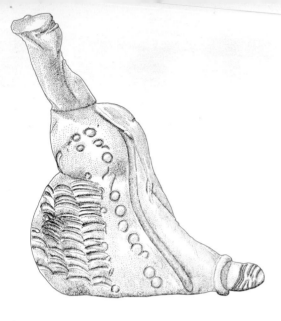

28 Clay figurine of 'mother goddess' type with impressed decoration from Tepe Sarab near Kermanshah

in the Zagros region in the seventh millennium BC at a time when other settlements, such as Jarmo were still pre-ceramic. Towards the end of Jarmo we first witness the adoption (or import) of pottery from the Kermanshah area, which is followed by a north-western group of coarser unpainted wares, ancestral or related to the earliest pottery of Hassuna. Other sites in the region, like Tell Shimshara preserved the pre-pottery tradition until the later Hassuna, or Samarra phase.

Cyprus in the Aceramic period: the Khirokitia culture

As far as we know Cyprus has always been an island, at least since the appearance of man in the Near East. Although it faces the south coast of Anatolia on the one hand, and that of Syria and the Lebanon on the other – both areas rich in palaeolithic remains – cave explorations have not yet been carried out in Cyprus. At the moment the earliest known culture – the aceramic of Khirokitia – is dated by the C-14 method to the sixth millennium BC (6020, 5850 and 5800 BC). In spite of this comparatively late date – perhaps the natural result of its comparative isolation – this culture in many respects resembles such Natufian sites as Ain Mallaha or Pre-Pottery A Jericho. The origins of the culture are utterly unknown, but earlier phases remain to be discovered, if not in Cyprus itself, then somewhere on the Asiatic mainland. Its distribution roughly covers the island and the import of obsidian points to contact with Anatolia. The discovery of a site of this period at the very end of the dagger-like Karpas peninsula is significant, for it points straight at the mouth of the Calycadnus valley, the old trade route from the Anatolian Plateau to the Mediterranean coast. It also points to Ras Shamra, another early maritime site in north Syria and to the Amuq (plain of Antioch) where a stone vessel of Khirokitia type was found in levels of the Amuq A period (before 6000 BC). Seafaring was evidently established at this period and one of the sites, Petra tou Limniti, was established on a small island in Morphou Bay.

Two features of the culture have no parallels elsewhere; a flint industry of peculiar type which is not microlithic, possibly a descendant of the Upper Palaeolithic, and secondly a round-headed (brachycephalic) population at Khirokitia itself, perhaps the result of isolation or a habit of cranial deformation.

Khirokitia is not a mound, but a hill site about 250 metres in diameter situated within a bend of the Maroniou river. It commands a view down to the south coast, which is a few miles away. A paved stone road running for about 200 metres through the settlement was traced leading down the hill towards the river. Forty-eight round houses of tholos type were excavated, a small proportion of the entire settlement, which may have contained a thousand houses and a population running into the thousands, for Khirokitia was evidently more than a village. Three main levels of buildings were found and the extremely solid construction of the houses indicates a considerable duration of the settlement.

Ill. 29

These round houses, varying in diameter from 3 to 4 and 7 to 8 metres, frequently had double walls, built of local limestone. Their superstructure consisted of a dome of stone, brick or light materials. In the larger houses two solid stone pillars probably supported an upper storey or wooden floor, reached by a ladder and it was here that people probably slept. Similar arrangements prevailed in the workshops of Beidha. Hearths, platforms for sleeping, and pits in the floor are frequent. Seats, windows and cupboards were found in the wall or in the stone pillars. The doorways had high thresholds, to keep out rain and mud, and a few stone steps led down into the room. Several compounds were found consisting of one large beehive house, and several others used as kitchens, workshops for grinding corn, etc. Courtyards were often paved with flat stones and circular tables show where the food was eaten. Some corridors appear to have been roofed and access to the courtyards was gained by ramps leading from the central street. The general impression is one of great efficiency and good organization.

These people practised burial among the houses or below the floors, and single contracted burials appear to have been the rule. Objects were deposited with the dead; stone bowls, frequently ceremonially broken, and necklaces with women, and pins and other offerings with men or children. From the rich burial gifts of the women it may be deduced that they were man's equal.

Something is known about the dress of these Neolithic people. Weaving is attested by the presence of spindle-whorls and garments were probably of wool. They were fastened with bone pins, and sewn with needles. Personal ornament is represented by stone beads, pendants and bracelets; and necklaces of dentalia shells, carnelian and greyish-green pikrite. Bone was used for handles of stone tools, for awls, pins and needles. Maces of polished stone were used as weapons.

Ill. 30

29 Reconstruction of the Early Neolithic settlement of Khirokitia in Cyprus showing domed houses, corridors, workshops and main road leading through the settlement

The polished stone industry was highly developed. In the lowest building level some attempts were made to produce clay pots, without apparent success. Spouted stone bowls of greenish-grey andesite – a local stone – and shallow dishes of round, square or roughly oblong shapes are the most common forms. Many of these are up to a foot in length. They are frequently plain but some of the finest are decorated with incisions or with plastic bands, rows of knobs and ribs sometimes reminiscent of wooden vessels or basketry. Some of the bowls have handles with thumb grips, like the later horned handles; others are ornamented with human or animal heads (sheep and bulls). Shallow round dishes, like those of Ain Mallaha or Jericho B, may have been used as lamps.

Figurines are not uncommon – there are stone standing figures with schematized heads and no indication of sex,

Ill. 31

Ill. 32

30–32 Necklace of carnelian beads and tusk-shaped dentalia shells from a woman's grave in Khirokitia. Right, spouted bowl and basin of andesite, a volcanic stone. Note the decoration on the basin, probably inspired by basket work, and the two holes indicating an ancient repair

and there is one fine woman's head in unbaked clay. Engraved or carved pebbles of uncertain use are common.

Of the economy of the Khirokitia settlement we know but little; no actual grain was found, but sickle blades, querns and grinding stones abound. There is evidence for domesticated sheep and goats and possibly pig. Apart from obsidian, only local materials were used.

The end of the culture is as mysterious as its beginning – Khirokitia and other sites were deserted and only at Troulli on the north coast is the next stage represented stratigraphically on top of the earlier remains. This phase (Neolithic I B) is characterized by the first pottery, painted in red on cream, highly burnished and probably closely related to the Hacılar I ware (c. 5250–5000 BC) of south-western Anatolia, whence the newcomers may have come.

CHAPTER FOUR

The Ceramic Neolithic Period in Syria the Lebanon and Palestine

We have seen how in the seventh millennium the Syrian tradition with rectangular architecture and plaster floors overrode the native Natufian Palestinian tradition with round house complexes. From the beginning of the sixth millennium or the end of the seventh, another northern tradition, ultimately derived from the Anatolian Plateau, introduced the art of making pottery and baked clay figurines. These changes did not come about in the way of trade, but involved the movement of groups of population. Many new settlements were founded and elsewhere newcomers mixed with the local population along the old obsidian trade route. The new cultures were not copied slavishly and became transformed and local variations flourished. It is too early to say whether the stone industries, especially in the north, did not continue the tradition of the late pre-ceramic period. The archaeological evidence for the period is uneven and only at Byblos was a large part of the settlement cleared. At every other site (Amuq, Ras Shamra, etc.) one is dealing with restricted soundings.

Where remains of buildings have come to light, rectangular plans are the rule, with the exception of Jericho where subterranean round huts are characteristic. The Jericho Pottery Neolithic shows signs of being of

33–34 Limestone pebble figurine and flint lancehead from Early Neolithic Byblos

somewhat later date, when such primitive ways of living become common.

The Byblos Early Neolithic settlement was located on a consolidated sand dune on the coast, which offered adequate defence. The houses were freestanding with plenty of open space and scattered on either side of a deep wadi. Most are small and have rectangular plans with stone foundations which bore a light superstructure, and they had white plaster floors which were frequently renewed. Some houses have more than one room, the second chamber being smaller, but one building at least was of impressive dimensions with a room not less than 10 metres in length. Plenty of evidence exists for a minimum of four to five successive building-levels. There are few interior fittings; a raised platform or seat occurs in most houses, but hearths are less easy to identify. The dead were buried inside the settlement and contracted burial was the rule. Sometimes bone piles are found next to intact burials, suggesting a rearrangement of earlier ones, as at Çatal Hüyük. Burial gifts consist of pottery, weapons and trinkets. The settlement was large and there would have been several hundred houses. Little is known of their economy, but wheat (and barley?) were grown and domesticated animals were probably kept. Hunting and fishing supplemented the larder. Weaving and spinning is indicated by the numerous spindle whorls; leatherwork by the bone awls. Stone pebble-like figurines are characteristic of Early Neolithic Byblos. Little can be added from other sites to this picture; in the Amuq A culture emmer wheat and hulled barley were grown and domesticated goat and pig are attested. Hunting was still common everywhere, as is clear from the stone industry, which is rich in flint spear or lanceheads, daggers and knives, and arrowheads. Obsidian was much more sparsely used, even in the Amuq. In the north, fully polished axes were made in greenstone; in the south,

Ill. 34

35–36   Early Neolithic dark burnished pottery from Byblos, decorated with cardium shell combing

where this material was not available, chipped flint axes with polished bits took their place. Miniature axes in fine green stones came from the north with the obsidian. Flint sickle-blades with coarsely serrated edges are characteristic of the Byblos Early Neolithic culture.

It is, however, in the pottery that regional peculiarities are most marked. In contrast to the undecorated burnished ware of the Anatolian Plateau, all the secondary neolithic cultures from Cilicia to Palestine show a distinct taste for decoration.

Ills. 35, 36

Although most of the pottery is undecorated, nail or shell (*murex*) impressed patterns, frequently rouletted, occur round the mouths of globular or squat hole-mouth jars in the neolithic of Mersin and Tarsus.

Other forms of decoration include incisions, pushed up triangles or ovals and excisions, which form a textured surface covering the vessel, and pointillé impressions. These forms of decoration are found on monochrome burnished wares, which vary in colour from greyish black, brown, chocolate, red and buff. The pottery is very well made, thin, hard-fired and tempered with grit; only in the buff or pinkish coarse ware is some straw temper in evidence.

59

In the Amuq A culture, very similar wares are found, but shapes differ and the impressed ornament is most often produced on a red washed ware, which does not occur in Cilicia. At Ras Shamra (VB) on the Syrian coast, most of the burnished ware is red, but some is brown and black. Ornament is rare; shapes are globular and poorly baked coarse ware is common as in the Amuq. However, two new classes of pottery appear, which have no parallels in Anatolia or Cilicia and represent local adaptations. One of these also found in Early Neolithic Byblos and in the Beqa'a consists of the northern monochrome ware, coated with a white lime-plaster slip on exterior, or interior or both. Useless on pottery, this may be an adaptation derived from earlier techniques for making a vessel of wood, basketry or skin watertight and fire-resistant.

The other uses a chalky material mixed with grits and straw to make large 'plaster' bowls and basins on a low foot or hollow base. The thickness of the walls, and the white material are strongly reminiscent of the pre-pottery limestone bowls and plates used in the previous period. This peculiar Syrian ware has been found from Ras Shamra and Tell Sukas to Tell Ramad near Damascus always in the earliest layers of the period. These two white wares proved unsatisfactory and their use did not last long. Farther south in the Early Neolithic of Lebanon, a vigorous culture is distributed from Tabbat el Hammam to Sidon, almost without any interruption in occupation from Tripoli to Sidon, but equally known inland where Byblos is the principal site. Its pottery shows greater variety of decoration than any other so far known in this period. Plain grey and brown burnished ware is in the minority and pink, amber coloured, buff and cream wares with burnished rims, globular or hemispherical shapes predominate. Below the rims, grooved or incised with a herringbone pattern between horizontal lines, the bodies of pots are decorated with combed patterns made by

dragging a ribbed shell over the surface of the pot. Others are ornamented with incisions, gouged patterns and cord impressions, all producing a textured surface which gives one the impression of imitating basketry, such as must have been in common use in the previous aceramic period. Almost identical pottery was found at Tell Abu Zureiq, Hazorea, Tell Kibri in the Esdraelon valley of north Palestine, as well as at Tell Sheikh Ali II, south of Lake Galilee, at Tell Ramad near Damascus and at Tell Batashi near Jaffa in the coastal plain. This pottery suggests an extension of the Byblos Early Neolithic culture inland and along the coast, and even here some dark burnished sherds show the strength of the Anatolian tradition.

Farther south another offshoot of a somewhat later phase of the Byblos Neolithic (Middle Neolithic) is found in the Jordan valley. This culture is known as the Yarmukian. Pottery shapes are more developed, jars with collar necks and handles and flat bases now appear. The pottery is coated with a red wash – as at Byblos – and ornamented with incised or combed herringbone patterns, on reserve (buff) ground. The stone industry shows strong links with Middle Neolithic Byblos and among figurines, pebbles with incised features, as in Early Neolithic Byblos are now combined with naturalistic clay figures with prominent eyes, noses and lips. Both pebble figurines and clay figures show ultimate relation to Anatolian types of Hacılar VI (which ended *c.* 5600 BC).

Ill. 37

Very similar shapes are found in the Jericho Pottery Neolithic A and B cultures, a complex difficult to disentangle and characterized by subterranean houses of circular shape. The B pottery shows incised herringbone patterns sometimes associated with red washed surfaces as in the Yarmukian, but the A pottery is painted red on a cream ground and burnished. The techniques between reserve slipped wares and painted wares are closely related, and it is not necessary to invoke a movement of new people to bring painted pottery from the north.

These southern cultures were the result of further developments in north Syria. In the Amuq B culture and in Ras Shamra (V C *c.* 6000–5500 BC) the monochrome wares developed new and elegant shapes, such as carinated bowls, ornamented with incised decoration or pattern burnish which produced dark geometric patterns on a lighter background. The distribution of dark burnished ware covered the greater part of northernmost Syria and similar dark on light effects were obtained by painting in red on cream pottery. This earliest painted pottery was primitive compared to that of its neighbours in Cilicia, or the Anatolian and Iranian plateaux. Plain red washes were much more common and both red wares (often with reserve patterns) and pattern burnished ware are a feature of Middle Neolithic Byblos. Accompanying these wares in the north is a coarse ware, frequently incised which shows clear links with that of the sixth millennium Hassuna culture of north Iraq. A characteristic shape, the so-called husking tray occurs from Tell Shimshara in the east to Ras Shamra on the Syrian coast, but it remained unknown in Cilicia and in the Lebanon.

Cilician developments were altogether different; for here the dark wares now bear incised patterns like that of Sakçagözü, but pattern burnished ware is absent.

Finer light-coloured wares occur, often with pointillé design, soon to give way to red on cream painted wares, which are both more developed than the Syrian ones and which show the unmistakable influence of its even more developed northern neighbour, the Çatal Hüyük West culture on the Anatolian Plateau. Influence from Syria on Cilicia did not appear until the late sixth millennium with the arrival of a vigorous new culture, called Halaf.

CHAPTER FIVE

The Cultures of Mesopotamia

The Hassuna and Samarra cultures of Northern Mesopotamia

While discussing the interesting sites of Jarmo and Tell Shimshara we have already drawn attention to two successive traditions of pottery making, an earlier Iranian one ('Jarmo painted pottery') and a later monochrome one which is related to the Hassuna 'neolithic' wares. The origin of the latter is by no means decided, but it is difficult to believe in view of Hassuna archaic wares, with and without incisions, found as far west as the north Syrian coast, that this tradition originated at the remote village of Jarmo or thereabouts in Kurdistan. The total absence of stone bowls and bracelets, or of a microlithic tradition, associated with Jarmo and Tell Shimshara in the Zagros region on the one hand and the totally different stone-industry with a sprinkling of obsidian projectile points of Anatolian type on the other, point, in my opinion conclusively to a more western origin. Such an origin is of course further suggested by the distribution of early Hassuna features as far west as the Mediterranean coast and the subsequent distribution of two later cultures its successors, Samarra and Halaf, which were equally widespread in distribution. Moreover, there is

38, 39   Alabaster statuettes with inlaid eyes and caps of bitumen from graves at Tell es Sawwan. Beginning of the Hassuna period

very little to link the early Hassuna pottery to its Iranian neighbours (Jarmo painted, Tell Sarab or Hajji Firuz); the shapes are western (Syria comes nearest) and the early red on buff painted ware is, lacking intermediate types, closest to Mersin. For what it is worth, the present writer would expect the origins of the Hassuna ware to lie somewhere in the hill region half way between Mosul and Aleppo, in the region of 'Turkish Mesopotamia' the region of Mardin and Diyarbekir. Here too, lies the suspected homeland of the Halaf culture and numerous other problems in Mesopotamian and Syrian archaeology may be solved by exploration and excavation in this perhaps vitally important 'third region', half way between the 'Zagros zone' and the 'Anatolian-Levant region'. At the moment, all this is conjecture, but it is somewhere in this region around Chagar Bazar in the Khabur valley that the distribution of the eastern, or Iraqi Hassuna painted wares and the western, or Syrian pattern burnished wares meet.

Whatever its origins may be, the Hassuna culture as such is known only in north Iraq. After its initial phases with monochrome cream pottery, found in three superimposed camp sites (Ia–Ic), its full development (II–IV) saw rectangular planned small houses of several rooms each, neatly built in pisé with reed mats covering the floors, hearths and ovens, storage pits lined with bitumen and occasional burials in pits. Pottery showed three main classes; plain coarse ware; plain ware with incision, red on cream painted ware and painted and incised ware. These gradually developed and became more sophisticated as is indicated by the prefixes of 'archaic' and 'standard'. From building-level IV (c. 5500 BC?) onwards a new painted pottery appears, perhaps imported. This is far more developed and is known as Samarra ware. Painted and painted-and-incised variants are found together. A naturalistic element portraying animals and

40   Mesopotamian painted pottery typology. *a–g*, Hassuna ware; *h–j*, Samarra ware; *k–m*, Hajji Muhammad ware

human beings, appears for the first time in Mesopotamia and more developed forms of composition are found, especially on the interior of large open bowls. Shapes change; pedestals are introduced; effigy figures showing human beings in relief occur on pots. Samarra pottery is common in north Syria and its arrival precedes or coincides with that of the Halaf culture there, *i.e.* somewhere around 5400 B C. Numerous sites show elements of both cultures side by side, but the origin of the Samarra culture is as disputed as that of Hassuna or Halaf. Some scholars have argued for an Iranian origin whereas others took Samarra ware as a development of the Hassuna culture. Neither view can now be seriously maintained; Iranian cultures probably borrowed motifs from the Samarran, which became well established in the hills (Tell Shimshara) and, had Samarra been a straight development from Hassuna, one would not have expected such a marked difference from the Hassuna pottery.

But for the pottery very little is known of the culture: mud-brick architecture is associated with it at Baghuz and in this western outpost certain types of stone tools appear which link it to Syria and Palestine. Metal has been reported from Samarra itself, and though doubt has been expressed about it, it would not surprise one at this period, when Anatolian metalsmiths had already learnt to produce mace-heads and bracelets of pure copper.

An important feature of the Hassuna and Samarra period is the establishment of settlements in areas where the annual rainfall is insufficient to practise dry farming. We must therefore infer that irrigation methods were used. Samarran influence has been established in two cultures, situated even farther south; the Jaffarabad I or Susiana I culture in Khuzistan and that of Eridu in the deep south of lower Mesopotamia.

In the Susa area we even find beside distinctive painted pottery monochrome wares of early Hassuna type and it

Ills. 40, 41

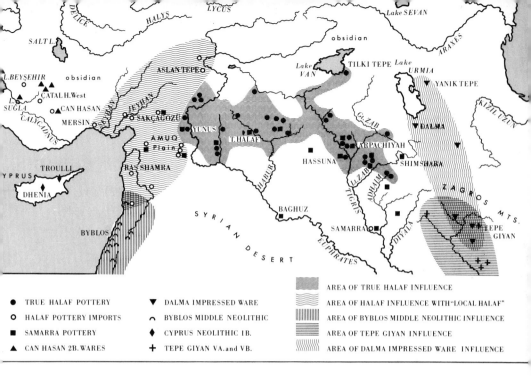

TRUE HALAF POTTERY   ●   DALMA IMPRESSED WARE ▼   AREA OF TRUE HALAF INFLUENCE

HALAF POTTERY IMPORTS   ○   BYBLOS MIDDLE NEOLITHIC ∩   AREA OF HALAF INFLUENCE WITH "LOCAL HALAF"

SAMARRA POTTERY   ■   CYPRUS NEOLITHIC IB. ◆   AREA OF BYBLOS MIDDLE NEOLITHIC INFLUENCE

CAN HASAN 2B. WARES   ▲   TEPE GIYAN VA. and VB. +   AREA OF TEPE GIYAN INFLUENCE

AREA OF DALMA IMPRESSED WARE INFLUENCE

41   The distribution of Halaf and Samarra wares in the Near East

is not impossible that this was the first pottery in the area (just as at Matarra, south of Kirkuk). One wonders whether this Hassuna monochrome archaic (or neolithic), also found in the uppermost levels at Jarmo and which now has a distribution from Ras Shamra to Susa, is not in fact the earliest pottery of this vast lowland area, and the basis on which local painted potteries developed. In Susiana, the first painted pottery shows numerous similarities to the Samarra culture, both in shape and design. Particularly common are patterns left in reserve which contrasts with the linear style of Samarra. Naturalistic schemes characteristic of Samarra, are not found.

The Eridu and Hajji Muhammad cultures of Southern Mesopotamia

At Eridu the lowest building levels XVIII–XV showed small houses and shrines, built of mud-brick with rectangular plans. The Eridu pottery, though stylistically akin to Samarra, has a strong local character. Bowls, plates, jars and beakers are the most common shapes; the pottery is fine and decorated in mat brownish black paint on a cream slip. Geometric patterns prevail, with fine centre pieces on large bowls. Although reserve patterns are in use, there is little in common between Susiana A and Eridu ware and the latter is probably somewhat later in date (*c*. 5000 BC).

The next phase, Hajji Muhammad, in southern Mesopotamia is of particular importance in that it provides the ancestor for the 'Ubaid culture (fully fledged by *c*. 4350 BC). Its beginning may perhaps be dated to *c*. 4750 BC or earlier and both Eridu and Ras al Amiya show five successive building-levels. Architectural remains are of the utmost simplicity, but the distribution of the culture is of considerable interest. It now covers most of southern Mesopotamia, but it is even better represented in Susiana (A and especially B culture) at Tepe Jowi, Ali Kosh, and numerous other mounds; as well as in the highlands of Luristan (*e.g.* Kozaragan). The links are so strong that movement of people must have been involved between the Luristan uplands and lower Mesopotamia and new evidence suggests that it descended from the Iranian mountains into the plain. Indirect contact with the new Halaf province in the north is amply attested by new shapes, glaze paint and patterns. The Hajji Muhammad pottery is decorated with glaze paint (rarely in mat paint) of dark brown, dark violet, dark green or bright red colour, sometimes with added incised patterns. Motifs are almost exclusively geometric, very 'busy' and often with reserve patterns. Many of the shapes are those familiar in the Halaf repertoire, but others are local. The presence of coarse ware with a strong straw temper again points to western Iran since it is not common in Mesopotamia.

CHAPTER SIX

The Cultures of Northern Iran

The Tepe Giyan V culture

A glance at the map suggests that the Tepe Giyan V culture in the central Zagros area may have played an important role in the transmission of culture between the Samarra and later Halaf regions north of the Diyala and those of Susiana. Not only did this culture control the 'Persian gates', the highway from Mesopotamia to Kermanshah and Hamadan, but also that from north Mesopotamia to Khuzistan for the desert between the Diyala and Khuzistan has shown no trace of any prehistoric occupation or the existence of a trade route along the solid mountain wall of the Kabir Kuh. The importance of the Giyan V culture is evident from the number of sites and its richly painted pottery. Giyan V A, the earliest phase, shows resemblances to Samarra and Jaffarabad; V B to Hajji Muhammad and Jowi and V C and D to 'Ubaid. Unfortunately nothing is known of the culture except its painted pottery and its distribution.

A radiocarbon date of 4039 BC from Tepe Siyahbid in the plain of Kermanshah presumably dates a phase contemporary with Dalma impressed ware.

Dalma Impressed Ware

Ill. 42

The recent discovery of a new sort of unpainted pottery in western Iran, the surface of which is decorated with impressions made with tubes, combs, sticks and fingers, or pinching and knobbing raises new problems. At Dalma Tepe in the plain of Solduz it overlies a layer with painted wares, dated by C-14 to 4216 BC, a date which compares well with that of Tell Siyahbid where the same pottery has been found. Its distribution is even wider and ranges from Yanik Tepe near Tabriz to Khorramabad, south of Giyan. Its relation to the Giyan V sequence is still unknown.

Pottery of this sort was hitherto unknown in Iran, but it may be compared to the incised simple wares of Matarrah and Hassuna; the incised and impressed wares of Cilicia, Syria, Lebanon and Palestine, or those of Thessaly, Macedonia and the Balkans (the Starčevo complex). All have one feature in common; they are all secondary neolithic cultures and the textured surfaces of the vessels may have been produced to imitate basketry. Even in the Halaf culture (earlier than or contemporary with Dalma) basketry imitations are found, produced by ribbed and grooved pottery, sometimes with paint added. The full implications of the appearance of this pottery are not yet known but it is not impossible that it marks an expansion of a less advanced element, from Iranian Kurdistan, a region where painted pottery cultures have not yet been established.

Ill. 43

This pottery follows another painted one at Dalma Tepe near Hasanlu. The Dalma painted ware is one of the finest products of Azerbaijan and, like its predecessor the Hajji Firuz ware, so far known only from the immediate region around Lake Urmia. Heavily tempered with straw (an Iranian characteristic) the Dalma painted ware is painted in purplish black on cream, and interiors are coated with a maroon red slip. Burnishing is common;

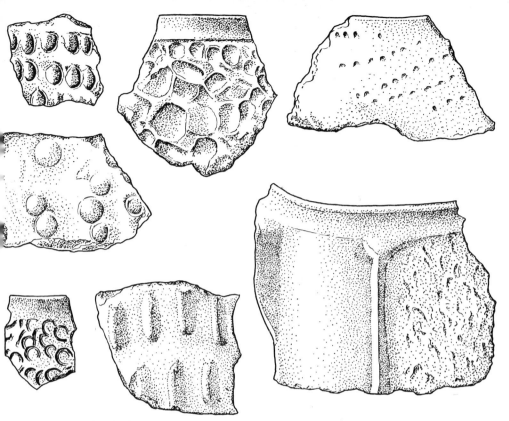

42 Unpainted Dalma impressed ware from Iranian Azerbaijan

jars, bowls and beakers are the most common shapes and plain ware also occurs. Small rooms were grouped around a courtyard which contained hearths, storage bins for food and pottery. Chert was more common than imported obsidian; weaving and spinning are attested by whorls and loom weights. The origin of the culture – roughly contemporary with Halaf to the west – is obscure.

The Hajji Firuz culture

The Dalma culture succeeded that known as Hajji Firuz from another small mound near Hasanlu, south of Lake Urmia. At least six superimposed building-levels were cleared which were roughly contemporary with the Hassuna and Samarra cultures (and with Hacilar V-I).

43 Painted Dalma pottery from Iranian Azerbaijan. The first pot, above left, earlier Hajji Firuz ware

Again houses of rectangular plan were built of packed mud and set around an open courtyard, containing the open hearths and large storage vessels. The second village from the top was burned and produced a radiocarbon date of 5152 BC. A massacre of the population had taken place and three mass graves with twenty-eight individuals and much pottery, plain, painted and straw tempered, some polished celts and flint blades were found. The dead had evidently been buried by the survivors and red ochre was powdered over the burials. The pottery of Hajji Firuz is simple and poorly fired. The plain pottery shows few shapes; the painted pottery in a fugitive red on cream or a few light pink designs. At Yanik Tepe near Tabriz several layers with only plain pottery may represent the beginning of the culture which could not be reached since

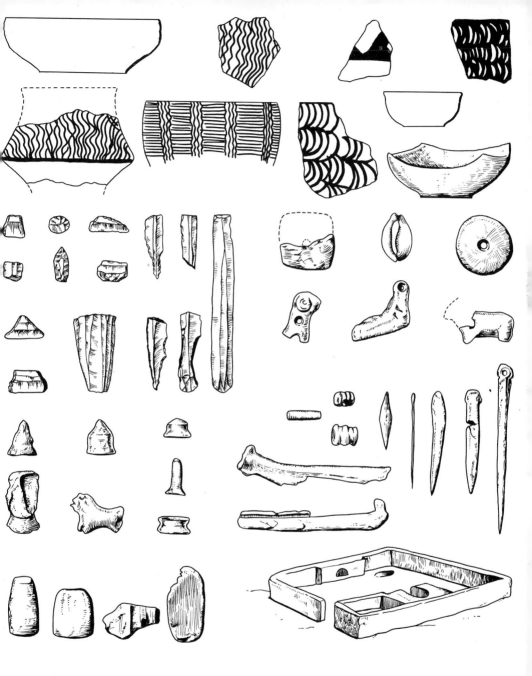

44 Typical assemblage of the Jeitun culture in western Turkestan. Below right, an example of a house with a walled courtyard

45, 46 A Siyalk III beaker, *c*. 4000 BC, decorated with a lively and free design characteristic of Iranian pottery of the period. Opposite, earlier Siyalk pottery which is comparable with the black-on-red pottery from level II of the type site and contemporary with Samarra ware

the levels are below water at the type site. Alabaster bowls, many bracelets and a few figurines (from Yanik Tepe) show the same north Zagros tradition as seen at contemporary Tepe Sarab, Tell Shimshara and the earlier aceramic cultures of Jarmo and Karim Shahir. An earlier level of Hajji Firuz was dated by C-14 to 5537 BC.

Iran beyond the Zagros Mountains

A number of early cultures have been found on the Iranian Plateau east of the Zagros Mountains; the Siyalk culture between Kashan and Teheran and lesser known cultures of Tepe Jarri B and Tell Muski in Fars, the region of Persepolis. Little was recorded about these cultures but their gaily painted pottery, the use of hammered copper in Siyalk II for small tools and trinkets and the use of pisé in Siyalk I and that of mud-brick in II for building. House plans are unknown and there are no C-14 dates so that the development is dated by comparison with Mesopotamia, a process that leaves much to be desired. The recent discoveries of a series of painted pottery cultures in the valleys between the Zagros ranges in Azerbaijan, Kurdistan and Luristan clearly demonstrates

that contacts with Mesopotamia or Elam were hardly of a direct nature, and the opening of the lapis lazuli route to eastern Afghanistan can at present only be dated to the 'Ubaid period. The size and the numbers of early settlements, however, leaves one in little doubt that farming was well established east of the Zagros, even if details are not available. Aceramic settlements have not yet been found, but in the sixth millennium painted pottery, buff in the south and red in the north is decorated in red, or brown and black paint. Neither shapes nor motifs of this earliest pottery owe anything to Mesopotamia and the pottery has a characteristic straw temper and often a slip. The Siyalk I pottery, which may be contemporary with Hassuna, is often decorated with patterns, which like the shapes, resemble baskets. A red and black monochrome ware is present. In Siyalk II and Cheshme Ali near Teheran, attractive geometric designs and also animals are painted in black on red and some links can be established with Samarra. An apparently unbroken development leads to the next phase, Siyalk III, roughly contemporary with Halaf (III, 1–2) and then 'Ubaid. Copper objects are now cast in moulds, stamp-seals with

Ill. 46

Ill. 45

geometric ornaments appear and in Siyalk III, 4 the potter's wheel occurs. Richly decorated goblets with geometric plant and animal motifs – including birds and leopards – are found and contemporary with Siyalk III, 1–2 we find a similar culture in the lowest level (I A) of Tepe Hissar near Damghan in eastern Iran.

Ill. 44

Typologically much earlier is the interesting settlement of Jeitun near Ashkhabad across the Turkmenian–Iranian border. Preceding the Anau I A culture, Jeitun may be as early as or earlier than Siyalk I and here again radiocarbon dates would be useful. The inhabitants of Jeitun were farmers and grew barley and wheat; they had domesticated sheep and goat, but most of their meat came from hunting bezoar, wild goat, sheep and gazelle. Their flint industry is microlithic but they made fully polished axes. Among the bone instruments 300 sickle handles are recorded. A straw-tempered pottery was made with simple shapes: cups, square bowls and cylindro-conical storage vessels, decorated in red-brown paint on a cream ground with vertical rows of wavy lines or brackets. Clay was also used for the manufacture of figurines and amulets were by no means rare. Far more remarkable is the architecture of an open village, over half of which was excavated. Nineteen houses, three small and sixteen large (varying in area from 20 to 35 square metres) stood by themselves each with its yard and farm and storage rooms adjoining. The houses were rectangular in plan, built of pisé, and consisted of one room each with a storage bin in one corner. A large square hearth was set near it along one of the walls with a projecting buttress containing a niche near floor-level just opposite. The buttress was painted red-brown or black, the floor covered with lime-plaster frequently stained red-brown as at Tepe Guran, Jericho, Beidha and Hacılar Aceramic. The discovery of Jeitun emphasizes only too clearly how little is known yet of early developments on the plateaux of Iran.

CHAPTER SEVEN

Anatolia

It may be said without undue exaggeration that Anatolia, long regarded as a barbarous fringe to the Fertile Crescent, has now been established as the most advanced centre of neolithic culture in the Near East. The neolithic civilization revealed at Çatal Hüyük shines like a supernova among the rather dim galaxy of contemporary peasant cultures. The comparison is apt for Çatal Hüyük with its successors, Hacılar, Çatal Hüyük West and Can Hasan, burnt itself out and left no permanent mark on the cultural development of Anatolia after *c.* 5000 B C. A faint afterglow may be detected in the Halaf culture of north Mesopotamia, but this too was doomed to disappear. Its most lasting effect was not felt in the Near East, but in Europe, for it was to this new continent that the neolithic cultures of Anatolia introduced the first beginnings of agriculture and stockbreeding and a cult of the Mother Goddess, the basis of our civilization.

In the preceding pages we have sketched the development of cultures throughout the Near East from their shadowy beginnings *c.* 10000 B C to the beginning of the Halaf culture (previously dated to *c.* 5000 B C, but perhaps considerably earlier). Following the terminology put forward at the beginning of the book, Mesolithic and Proto-Neolithic remains are clearly identifiable only in

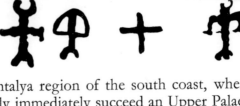

the Antalya region of the south coast, where they may possibly immediately succeed an Upper Palaeolithic with engravings on the walls of caves and art mobilier decorated with naturalistic forms and geometric ornament. The Belbaşı culture with its fine microliths may be regarded as Mesolithic and a northern equivalent to the Kebaran industries of Syria, the Lebanon and Palestine, whereas the probably later Beldibi culture (also with microliths, lunates, and perhaps rock paintings), compares typologically with the Proto-Neolithic Natufian. The presence of sickle blades lends substance to the theory of early agriculture, that is, reaping rather than sowing, but the main form of economy was evidently still the hunt.

In a country as unsuitable for agriculture as Pamphylia this causes little surprise. As no radiocarbon dates are available to establish the absolute date of the Belbaşı or Beldibi cultures (or the Upper Palaeolithic of the caves of Kara' In and Öküzlü' In) our only guide to chronology is provided by the occurrence of a primitive pottery at the very end of the top level (B) at Beldibi. Almost identical pottery was found stratified at Çatal Hüyük in Levels IX and X, which suggests a chronological link about 6500–6400 B C on the basis of radiocarbon dating. On the south coast then it is possible that the Proto-Neolithic lasted until the middle of the seventh millennium. If we accept this inference, one cannot escape the conclusion that the Pamphylian coast was as retarded in culture then as it was to be for thousands of years to come. Whereas the people at Beldibi who get their pottery, or the technique of making it from the plateau (the reverse process is unimaginable) still lived in rock-shelters, a fully developed town, Çatal Hüyük, already existed on the Anatolian Plateau. The plateau sequence – still incompletely known – may well turn out to be different from the coastal one. The importance of the

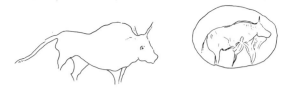

47, 48 Rock paintings from Beldibi, near Antalya. Right, Upper Palaeolithic engravings on rock, top left from Öküzlü' In cave and Beldibi, pebble from Kara' In cave, Antalya region, south Turkish coast

discoveries of Professor K. Kökten and Dr E. Bostanci in the Antalya area cannot be over-emphasized for they have shown for the first time that Upper Palaeolithic art of the west European type existed in Anatolia. It is to be expected that the people who produced the Neolithic Revolution in the Near East are probably to a great extent of Upper Palaeolithic stock, and some anthropologists believe that the Eurafrican race, the earliest strain represented in Proto-Neolithic cemeteries, represent descendants of Upper Palaeolithic man of Europe. It is the changeover from hunting and gathering to food production and food preservation that is probably responsible for the disappearance of the old animal art, but this was probably a very gradual affair and by no means universal. We have already seen a faint survival in the Natufian of Palestine but it was far more marked in the wall-paintings and plaster engravings of the neolithic site of Çatal Hüyük. There this naturalistic art survived until the middle of the fifty-eighth century BC, but it is no longer found in the later cultures of Hacılar or Can Hasan, where its place is taken by geometrically painted pottery, itself

Ills. 47, 48

derived from the symbolic and geometric art which accompanied the naturalistic.

In southern Anatolia there is therefore evidence for a development, however tenuous at present, from the Upper Palaeolithic to the Neolithic and in this respect Anatolia is unique.

At the moment the earliest evidence for settled communities on the plateau is provided by only two neolithic sites; an Aceramic village at Hacılar and the great site of Çatal Hüyük. Radiocarbon dating suggests that the date of the Hacılar village must be placed *c*. 7000 B C. Founded on virgin soil, a small·village with rectangular rooms, built of mud-brick on stone foundations, it lasted through seven phases of occupation before it was deserted. Tidily constructed hearths and ovens were grouped in an open courtyard with grain boxes made of plaster near at hand. Postholes suggest the presence of awnings and fences in the open court which was separated from the dwelling quarters by a metre thick wall. Houses appear to have consisted of a large room without interior fittings, but with carefully plastered floors and walls, laid on a pebble

Ill. 49

base. The plaster was frequently stained red and burnished or decorated with elementary geometric designs in red on cream. The walls were extremely denuded so that it is unknown whether wall-paintings once existed above a red dado. No doorways were found. Smaller rooms, sometimes provided with hearths or ovens surrounded the main room. It is possible that, as at Çatal Hüyük, entry was from the roof only.

Pottery was unknown and clay figurines have not been found. A few fragments show that marble bowls were in use and basketry, skins, wood and leather were probably used. Bone awls, flint and imported obsidian tools were found, mainly sickle blades and one polished axe. No burials were found within the settlement, but human crania were set up on floors, which suggests an ancestor cult. Among the animal bones, the remains of meals, sheep or goat, cattle and deer are present, no proof was found for domestication with the exception of a dog. Agriculture was practised as is shown by the remains of two-row hulled barley, emmer, wild einkorn and lentils from Level V, dated by C-14 to 7040 B C (higher half life).

The simplicity of the Aceramic settlement at Hacılar is reminiscent of Jericho Pre-Pottery Neolithic B or Jarmo, but it provides a strong contrast to the wealthy town-site of Çatal Hüyük, situated on a river in the alluvial plain of Konya some two hundred miles farther east.

Çatal Hüyük

With its thirty-two acres, Çatal Hüyük is easily the largest neolithic site in the Near East, but of this vast surface only an area covering an acre of the priestly quarter has yet been excavated. Twelve successive building-levels (O–X), covering the millennium from *c.* 6500 to 5650 B C, according to a series of fourteen radiocarbon dates, show a steady and unbroken development of culture. The late building-levels from Level VI A onward show an increase in disastrous fires which shortened the time-span of these levels and necessitated a quicker rate of rebuilding. The architecture of Çatal Hüyük is remarkably stereotyped: houses and shrines were built of shaped mud-brick on brick foundations in the absence of stone. Plans are rectangular and each house has a storeroom added to it along one of its sides. Interior arrangements vary according to the requirements of lighting by means of small windows set high up in the wall below the eaves. Each house had only a single storey, the height of its own walls, and was entered from the roof by means of a wooden ladder placed against the south wall. The smoke from the hearth and the oven escaped through the same hole in the flat roof or through the unglazed windows. Some buildings were provided with a ventilation shaft as well. All

Painted plaster
floor from level II
of the Aceramic
village at Hacılar

communications took place over the roofs – which varied
in height – as the buildings rose in terraces up the slope
of the mound. Wooden ladders must have abounded on
the roofs as they do today in Anatolian villages, where a
great part of the life of the village goes on. Each room was
provided with at least two platforms of which the main
one was framed by wooden posts, plastered over and
painted red. A raised bench was placed at the far end of
the main platform. These served as divans for sitting,
working and sleeping and below them the dead were
buried. Mats covered the floors. Sanitation was out of
doors in ruined houses or small open courtyards which
also served as repositories for domestic rubbish, ashes and
broken bones and pottery. Animals were not kept within
the settlement, but were probably herded at night into
corrals situated on the edge of the settlement. Because of
the peculiar system of entry the outside of the settlement
presented a solid blank wall and further defences were
evidently deemed unnecessary. Defenders armed with

50 Wall-painting of a man and his dog hunting deer from level III, *c.* 5800 BC, at Çatal Hüyük. The only definite evidence for the domestication of the dog at this early period

51, 52 Reconstruction drawing and original wall-painting from a shrine at Çatal Hüyük level VII, *c.* 6200 BC, showing a volcanic eruption, probably of Hasan Dağ, and a view of a town, Çatal Hüyük (?), with houses rising terraces in the foreground

bow and arrow, slings and spears, were evidently a match for any marauding band that would dare attack the city and no traces of massacre have been found.

The economy of Çatal Hüyük was based on extensive agriculture, on stock breeding (sheep and cattle?) and on hunting wild cattle (*Bos primigenius*), Red deer, wild ass, boar, and leopards. Fishing was relatively unimportant, but bird bones and eggshells are not uncommon. Wolves were killed (but not necessarily eaten), and a wall-painting shows a man accompanied by a dog, hunting deer. The standard of agriculture is amazing: emmer, einkorn, bread wheat, naked barley, pea, vetch and bitter vetch, were widely grown. Vegetable oil was obtained from crucifers and from almonds, acorn and pistachio. Hackberry seeds occur in great quanitites suggesting the production of hackberry wine, praised by Pliny and it may certainly be assumed that beer was also known.

Trade was another, if not the most important source of income for the inhabitants of Çatal Hüyük. The abundance of obsidian at this site, and its position relative to the source, the then active volcanoes of Karaca Dağ and Hasan Dağ at the eastern end of the plain strongly suggest that the city of Çatal Hüyük held the monopoly of the obsidian trade with the west of Anatolia, Cyprus and the Levant. A remarkable wall-painting from a shrine in Level VII shows a view of the town and a volcanic eruption, probably of Hasan Dağ, in the distance. Obsidian spearheads in prime condition are frequently found in groups of up to twenty-three specimens buried in a bag below the floor, where they were evidently stored as capital. In exchange for obsidian, the fine tabular flint of Syria was obtained and widely used for the manufacture of daggers and other tools. Sea shells, especially dentalia, were imported in great quantities from the Mediterranean for the manufacture of beads and stones of great variety were brought to the city for the manufacture of stone

Ill. 50

Ills. 51, 52

luxury vessels, beads and pendants, polishers, grinding stones, pounders, mortars and querns, or to be used (like alabaster and marble, black and brown limestone) for the manufacture of small cult statues. Greenstone occurs on a ridge in the plain and it was used for fully polished adzes and axes, and for jewellery. Ochres and other paints came from the hills around the plain together with fossil shells, lignite, copper and iron ores, native copper, cinnabar and galena. All these raw materials were used on the site, but the workshops have not yet been located. The standard of their technology is no less amazing: their obsidian and flint work with beautifully pressure flaked spear, lance and arrowheads in the former and daggers in the latter material leaves all other chipping in the Near East far behind. Mirrors were made of polished obsidian, set in a fine lime-plaster to fit neatly into the hand; beads were made of a blue or green stone, apatite, with perforations too small for a modern needle; holes were drilled in obsidian pendants, inlay of one stone into another was practised, copper and lead beads, pendants and other trinkets were frequently made from smelted ores as early as Level IX and fine textiles (probably wool) were produced of such fine quality as no manufacturer could be ashamed of now. The wooden vessels that, together with basketry, took the place of pottery in the lower levels of the site, shows a variety of forms, a mastery of technique and a sophistication in taste that has no parallels elsewhere in the neolithic Near East. Pottery itself appears first in Levels X–IX (and was exported to Beldibi), but this primitive stuff evidently could not compete with the wooden or bone and antler vessels, or the basket and skin containers, which may have been in use since the Upper Palaeolithic. As a result no pottery was found in the priestly quarter excavated in Levels VIII–VI B and it was only at the end of Level VI A, c. 5900 BC that now technically greatly improved it was

Ills. 53, 55

Ill. 54

Ill. 56

Ill. 57

Ills. 63, 69

Ills. 58, 59

53, 54 A bifacially flaked obsidian arrowhead from Çatal Hüyük, one of a group of seven buried with a dead man in a bag. Above, a woman's grave in level VI, Çatal Hüyük with an obsidian mirror, an impression of a coiled basket (left) and a small basket with red ochre, mixed with fat to form 'rouge' (right)

finally accepted. Only Levels V–O are to be considered as fully ceramic at Çatal Hüyük, but even then the proto-types in wood and basketry influenced the greater part of the shapes until the end of the settlement. This is the so-called dark burnished ware but at Çatal Hüyük the dark colour is usually confined to the cooking pots and from Level V onwards buff wares appear (there are red ones as early as Level X). Mottling in attractive colours is common in Level IV and the first streaks of red paint occur in Levels III and II, but remain exceedingly rare. Not a single sherd was found with the rouletted, fingernail or shell-impressed ornament so common on its Cilician offshoots.

The people of Çatal Hüyük buried their dead below the platforms of their houses and shrines only after the flesh had been removed, probably for the sake of hygiene. The primary process of excarnation may have taken place in *Ills. 62, 65, 86* light structures, built of bundles of reeds and matting as

55, 56 Above, a ceremonial pressure-flaked flint dagger from a male burial in level VI, Çatal Hüyük. The bone handle is carved in the form of a serpent. *Ill. 56*, below, a necklace of blue or green apatite and amber-coloured stalactite calcite beads

57-59   Textile (wool?) enveloping the lower jaw of a burial from shrine E VI 5, Çatal Hüyük. *Ills. 58, 59*, below left, black burnished pottery from Çatal Hüyük level VI A, *c.* 5900 BC

Ill. 64
Ills. 69, 102

depicted on a wall of a shrine, or by means of vultures. The fleshless corpses were then collected, wrapped up in cloth, skins or matting and intra-murally buried previous to the annual redecoration of houses and shrines. Sometimes the remains were coated or painted with red ochre, cinnaber, or blue or green paint was applied to the neck or forehead. The dead were furnished with funerary gifts; women and children with jewellery; necklaces, armlets, bracelets and anklets, greenstone hoes (or adzes), bone spatulae and spoons, especially when women were buried with children. In the case of more prominent members of society obsidian mirrors, baskets with rouge and cosmetic spatulae were included. Male burials were accompanied by mace-heads, flint daggers, obsidian spear, lance or arrowheads, clay seals, bone hooks and eyes, and fasteners for belts. Textiles, wooden vessels and boxes are found with both sexes, but pottery or figurines are never found in the graves.

60, 61 Burial in a basket from level VI and a group of contracted burials from below the platforms of a shrine also in level VI, Çatal Hüyük

Until a full study is available, little can be said about the population except that they were dolichocephalic, of fair stature and thin boned. The majority of burials are those of women and children and few individuals appear to have reached middle age.

Art and religion

The discovery of forty shrines or sanctuaries distributed over nine building-levels at Çatal Hüyük gives one a unique picture of neolithic Anatolian religion. The shrines are of the same plan and structure as the houses, but are distinguished by their superior decoration or their contents. They are grouped within a complex of buildings and four to five rooms are usually served by a shrine. *Ill. 68* Continuity of cult can be demonstrated in a number of instances in the lower levels, where shrine was built upon shrine, but there are also exceptions where this is not the case. Numerous groups of statues in stone or baked clay

62–65   Above, a reconstruction of a shrine in level VII decorated with wall-paintings of vultures pecking at human bodies. *Ill. 63*, below left, a wooden box carved out of fir wood with lid from a burial in level VI (*cf. Ill. 69*), a human jaw lies close by. *Ill. 64*, below right, a baked clay stamp seal with stylized flower petals from a burial in level IV, *c.* 5850 BC. *Ill. 65*, opposite above, a second vulture shrine from level VII showing two vultures with human legs attacking a headless human body, *c.* 6150 BC

66, 67 Right, bead necklaces, bracelets of
various cut and polished stones, bone belt-
hooks (*cf. Ill. 102*), and eyes from levels VI
A and B. *Ill. 67*, below, a 'red-ochre burial' of
a woman with a band of deep red paint,
cinnabar or mercury oxide applied to the
skull. From level VI B, *c.* 6000 BC

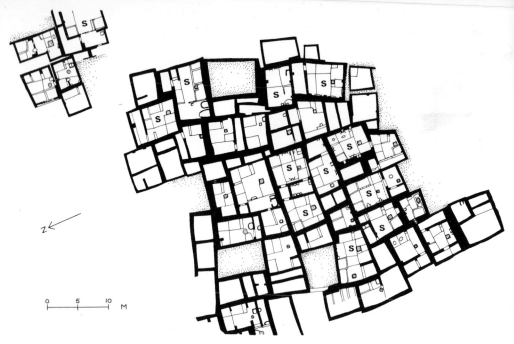

68   Plan of building-level VI B at Çatal Hüyük, *c.* 6000 B C. *s*, shrine

were found, as well as crude ex-voto figurines of seated human beings and animals. The latter are never found inside the shrines, but lie outside or are stuck into recesses in the wall, whereas the cult statues are found within the shrines. The statues allow us to recognize the main deities worshipped by neolithic people at Çatal Hüyük.

Ills. 73–75
The principal deity was a goddess who is shown in her three aspects, as a young woman, a mother giving birth or as an old woman, in one case accompanied by a bird of prey, probably a vulture. Simpler and more terrifying

Ill. 72
aspects show her semi-iconic as a stalactite or concretion with a human head which probably emphasizes her chthonic aspects related to caves and underworld. One figure shows the twin goddess and a group of three

Ills. 70, 71
figures shows a girl, a woman and a boy god standing behind or riding leopards, the sacred animal of the goddess. A male deity also appears frequently in two aspects,

Ills. 77, 79
as a boy or adolescent, the son or paramour of the god-

92

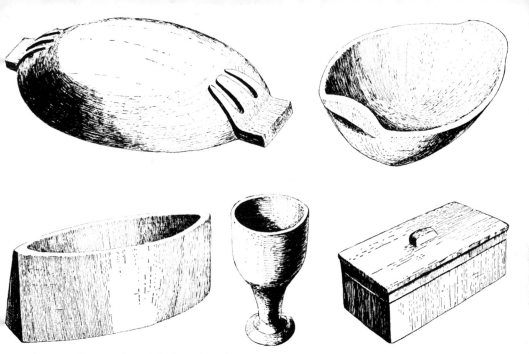

69 Wooden vessels mainly from burials in level VI at Çatal Hüyük

dess, or as an older god with a beard, frequently portrayed on a bull, the god's sacred animal. Groups of figures are rare. No other deities are recognizable, but groups of statues are always accompanied by limestone concretions, stalactites from caves and strange stones. *Ill. 78*
Ill. 76

In the decoration of shrines three different methods were employed:

i) Wall-paintings in natural colours (often polychrome) mixed with fat and painted with a brush on a fine white plaster, occur from Level X–III, but plain red panels continue into Level II.

These paintings were put up for religious use and were afterwards covered with plain white plaster. Frequently more than one layer of paintings are preserved.

ii) Reliefs, often of monumental size, up to 2 metres or more in height, modelled in plaster on bundles of straw, on wood, or on clay, and in the case of animal heads *Ills. 81, 83*

93

70–75　Ills. 70, 71, above, a boy-god riding on a leopard and a female deity standing behind a leopard. Ill. 72, below left, a limestone concretion with carved human head. Ill. 73, opposite left, a large baked clay figure of a goddess enthroned on two felines in the process of giving birth, from level II c. 5750 BC. The head is a restoration. Ill. 74, opposite right, a kneeling goddess in white marble found with the bird of prey (vulture?) Ill. 75

frequently incorporating the frontal bone and horn cores of bulls or rams. Levels IX–VI A.

iii) Figures, usually animals cut out of the plaster and part modelled or part cut-out; plain silhouettes or intaglio-like figures in sunk relief. Levels IX–VI A.

Finally there are groups or even rows of bull's horn-cores set in benches (Level VI only) or bull-pillars, stylized bull's heads incorporating the horns, set on the edges of platforms in shrines and houses alike, probably like the later horns of consecration to protect the inhabitants and ward off evil. These are first found in Level VII and continue right down to Level II.

In the plaster reliefs only the goddess is shown in anthropomorphic form, the male god, however, appears only as

76 Greenish-grey stone plaque with two figures in an embrace on the left and a mother and child on the right

77–79   A white marble statue of a seated god, wearing armlets and a cap made of leopard skin.
Ill. 78, centre, alabaster statue of a bearded god seated on a bull. *Ill. 79*, a white marble statue of
a young male deity. All from level VI, Çatal Hüyük

Ill. 83

Ills. 80, 86

a bull's or ram's head. The shrines were evidently the
scene of a fertility cult, the main aim of the religion being
the procreation of life, and the ensurance of its continuity
and abundance both in this life and next. Sexual symbol-
ism is absent and attention is drawn to the navel, preg-
nancy or scenes in which the goddess gives birth to a
bull's head or a ram's head. Frequently the two aspects
of the goddess are shown side by side or combined in a
twin figure, one of which is giving birth. Scenes of life on
one wall contrast with scenes of death on the other. A
huge bull's head is frequently found emerging from the
wall above a red painted niche, perhaps symbolic for the
netherworld. Other heads accompany the bull and breasts
are frequently shown in rows. In other cases woman's

80 Reconstruction of a shrine in level VI with a cut-out figure of a bull on the north wall and a bull and ram's head on the east wall. The wall beneath them is painted with a decoration of human hands.

breasts are carefully portrayed, but incorporate the lower jaws of wild boars, the skulls of fox, weasel or the griffon vulture, unmistakable symbols of death. Equally symbolic is the combination of bull's horn and woman's breast, both symbols of life. No two shrines are alike and the variations are bewildering; paintings combined with relief, cut out figures, painted red or black, together with reliefs and so on. The cut-out figures show bulls and cows, leopards, deer and a huge boar's head. In another instance the goddess is not represented but her place is taken by two leopards shown face to face, modelled in plaster and richly painted.

Ill. 81

The wall-paintings show a number of different subjects; besides plain panels of red (also found in houses) and occasionally black, there are numerous examples with geometric patterns, often of great intricacy, which resemble the gaily coloured Anatolian kilims (Levels X–III). Some even imitate the stitched borders and this suggests that they are copies of woven materials and not the prototypes from which kilim patterns were taken. Symbols such as hands, horns and crosses are frequently

97

81 A painted relief showing two leopards from a shrine in level VI, Çatal Hüyük, *c.* 6000 BC

Ill. 80

82 Painting of a dead man's head, from a shrine in level IV, *c.* 5825 BC

found in these paintings as befits their magical and protective function. Other paintings seem to consist entirely of symbols, most of which remain unintelligible to us. Paintings with human hands are frequent, either left in reserve on a red ground or painted in red, pink, grey or black, by themselves, or framing a central pattern of some complexity (Levels VII–VI A). A number of scenes are evidently related to the funerary cult: a fragmentary painting in Level IV shows a man probably carrying two human heads, of which only the male head is well preserved. A charnel house from a shrine in Level VI B has already been mentioned and in Level VII two great shrines show enormous vultures pecking at headless human corpses, whereas an earlier scene in Level VIII shows a man armed with a sling defending a corpse against two black vultures. Other buildings show great bulls painted in red or black, always on the north wall of the building, facing the Taurus Mountains (Levels IX, VII, VI and III).

Hunting scenes with numerous small human figures and Red deer occupy a shrine in Level III *c.* 5800 BC, the

83 Painted relief of a pregnant goddess, dressed and holding a veil from level VII, *c.* 6150 BC

84, 85 View of a bench in a shrine from level VI incorporating the horn cores of seven aurochs (wild bulls) and a reconstruction drawing of the complete shrine showing the bench and typical *bucrania*, pillars of brick with horn cores of the aurochs, symbol of the bull god

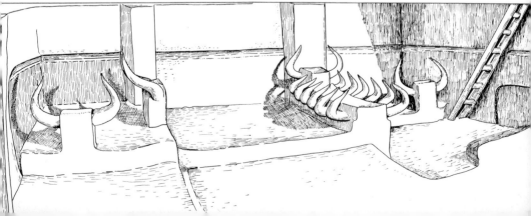

latest known at Çatal Hüyük. The decline in hunting and hunting equipment and probably the full domestication of cattle may have made the painting of hunting scenes, which were part of the ritual of the hunt, superfluous and they therefore disappear after Level III. This change in economy may also have affected the position of the male god *vis à vis* the great goddess. He is not represented among the nine statues from the shrine in Level II and in the Late Neolithic of Hacılar no single statue of the god is found by himself. At Çatal Hüyük II his birth and at Hacılar VI his mating with the goddess is shown, but his role has evidently been greatly diminished and his prestige has irreparably suffered.

Radiocarbon dates for Çatal Hüyük suggest that there is a slight chronological overlap between the end of the Çatal Hüyük (I–O) sequence and the 'Late Neolithic' of Hacılar (IX, VIII) and this is to some extent confirmed by a number of, perhaps only minor, features shared by these two sites, which it should be remembered are a good

two hundred miles apart. The first traces of painting on pottery occur at Çatal Hüyük III and II and thereafter Hacılar IX–VI, but such pieces remain in the minority. Light coloured wares are more common at the latter site than at the former, and tubular lug handles vertically placed appear sporadically at Çatal Hüyük II and I. At Hacılar they are common but here we now have a number of pots, including some with basket handles which are much more common at Çatal Hüyük. The stone industry of Çatal Hüyük II is debased and developing towards that of Hacılar and in both some microlithic elements now appear, although these are not even remotely similar. The clay figurines from Çatal Hüyük II show similar

positions to those of Hacılar and a goddess enthroned on leopards is closely related to figures from Hacılar VI, but facial features and hairstyles are quite different. Internal buttresses in architecture make their appearance in Çatal

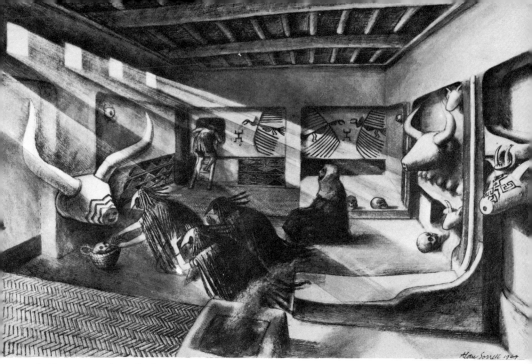

86 Reconstruction of a funerary rite, with priestesses disguised as vultures, taking place in a shrine in level VII at Çatal Hüyük, *c.* 6150 BC. It is based on the actual discovery of wall-paintings of vultures with human legs and human skulls on platforms below them found against the north wall, and skulls found in baskets below each large bull's head on the west and east walls

Hüyük II and in Hacılar VI, but house-plans and entry into the house are different and so are the burial habits. All this points to lines of development already fully diverged in the early sixth millennium BC and only further research can determine at what point in time Hacılar or rather its hypothetical predecessor the Kızılkaya culture, branched off from the parent stock. This culture, only known from surface finds in south-west Anatolia or from sporadic sherds in the Pamphylian caves, shows clear links in its ceramic repertoire to Çatal Hüyük, but not so in its stone industry from which the fine obsidian hunting equipment is conspicuously lacking. The direct descendant of the Çatal Hüyük culture probably lies buried below the western half of the mound across the river which is not yet excavated.

87 Scene of a Red deer hunt from the antechamber of a hunting shrine in level III, Çatal Hüyük, c. 5800 BC

Hacılar

Leaving aside the complicated issues which arise whenever an attempt is made to derive one culture from another, the short phase, hitherto called 'Late Neolithic' and lasting perhaps not more than a hundred years (5700–5600 BC) at Hacılar, produced some considerable archaeological remains. The remains of the first three phases, Levels IX–VII, are comparatively insignificant, but the final phase, Level VI, which was destroyed in a violent conflagration, was anything but insignificant. The remains of nine substantial houses arranged round two sides of a rectangular court were excavated. These houses were much larger than those of Çatal Hüyük and measured up to 10.5 metres in length and 6 metres in width. They were built of square bricks, with walls a metre thick and had stone foundations. They supported an upper storey, largely built of wood, and stout wooden posts held up the roof. A wide double doorway in the middle

Ill. 89

88 Anatolian pottery stages. Above, Early Neolithic monochrome pottery from Çatal Hüyük. Centre, Late Neolithic and early painted pottery, some with lug handles, from Hacılar. Below, painted pottery from the beginning of the early Chalcolithic period, also from Hacılar V, *c.* 5500 BC

of the long side of the building led into the room and facing the entrance a flat-topped oven stood against the back wall with a rectangular or square raised hearth immediately in front. Part of the room was screened off and the screen made of sticks covered with white lime-plaster, which also covered walls and floors, but was never painted. Platforms no longer exist, cupboards are placed in the thickness of the wall or built up in brick and plaster. An outdoor kitchen was placed to the right of the entrance and made of posts, laths and plaster and contained an oven, hearth, grinding stones and often grain boxes, made of plaster. In one case a flight of mud-brick steps led up to the second storey. Behind one of the houses in a small open court was a deep stone-lined well. The houses were built back to back in blocks and entered from courtyards or narrow lanes, but it is likely that the settlement was surrounded by a defensive wall. No special cult rooms were found, yet statuettes found in most houses suggest a domestic cult.

The economy of the period shows a great decline in hunting (and a corresponding absence in hunting weapons – only the mace and sling survive) but insufficient animal bones were found to be able to provide adequate proof for the domestication of cattle, sheep, goat and pig, although bones of these animals were found. Only the dog may definitely be said to be domesticated, nevertheless it would be most unusual if the other animals were still wild! Agriculture on the other hand was practised widely as dry farming, and carbonized deposits of emmer, einkorn, bread wheat, naked barley, Hacılar peas, bitter vetch, acorns and hackberry, were common-place. Sickles made of antler, sometimes still containing the small chert blades, occur in the houses together with graceful bone spatulae the handles of which end in animal heads. Bone carving was well developed and antler sleeves were used to hold polished stone axes, adzes and

Ill. 91

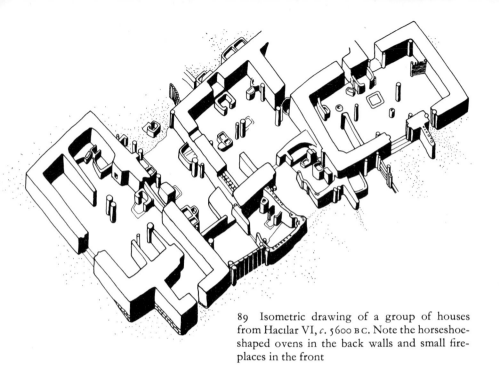

89 Isometric drawing of a group of houses from Hacılar VI, *c*. 5600 B C. Note the horseshoe-shaped ovens in the back walls and small fireplaces in the front

chisels made of greenstone, which is locally available. Articles of personal use include miniature mortars and pestles for cosmetics, red ochre, beads of various stones, pendants of mother-of-pearl, veined marble and apatite. Marbles and knuckle bones attest the playing of games. Impressions of basketry and weaving were found and biconical spindle-whorls appear. Copper is rare, but known, and haematite was used for polishers. A great number of raw materials not locally available show extensive trade with the south coast (sea shells), the Lake District (ochres, sulphur) and central Anatolia (obsidian, pumice stone). Obsidian is fairly rare, as a local buff or red chert was used for the manufacture of tools (mainly blades).

Pottery is abundant, thin-walled, hard-fired and brilliantly burnished. Light greys predominate in Levels IX and VIII and give way to fine reds, buffs and browns in VII and VI. Shapes are sophisticated and simple S-curves

90, 91 A drinking cup of red burnished ware in the form of a woman's head and bone spatulae with terminals in the form of animal heads

frequent, disc bases and vertically placed tubular lugs universal. These same bowl shapes occur in marble, sometimes of considerable size. Ritual vessels include recumbent and standing animals (deer, bull, pig), a cup in the form of a human head, and others are ornamented with bucrania, bull's or bear's heads or a human arm in relief. Painted pots remain great rarities, but the use of a red slip is well known.

Ills. 90, 92

Evidence for a domestic cult is provided by flat standing female figures made of baked clay or stone equivalents with incised eyes, nose, hair and chin and found in each house. Statuettes of baked clay, extremely well modelled, are accompanied by coarser figurines of the same material but provided with wooden peg heads. The statuettes portray the goddess and the male occurs only in a subsidiary role as child or paramour. The goddess is shown seated on one or two leopards or standing and holding a leopard cub. She occurs by herself, standing, seated, squatting, kneeling, lying down or accompanied by a child. She may be shown in the nude or wearing a bikini-like garment, an apron or a long striped dress, painted in white. In the younger aspect she wears her hair in pigtails and is usually scantily dressed, whereas the older figures are more often naked and have the hair

Ill. 93

Ill. 94

92 Ritual vessel in the shape of a recumbent deer from Hacılar VI

done up in a bun. Eyes are incised, but none have a mouth. The physical types appear to be depicted which may reflect the two dolichocephalic races recognized by the late Professor M. Şenyürek in the skeletons from Hacılar; the robust Eurafrican race and the more gracile Proto-Mediterranean race. These naturalistic statues serve as a link between those of Çatal Hüyük and the later, larger and more conventionalized group from Hacılar V–II.

After the destruction of Hacılar VI, *c.* 5600 B C, occupation continued and the 'Late Neolithic' gradually developed into the 'Early Chalcolithic' phase, the main characteristic of which is the use of painted pottery. This was a gradual affair and in Level V, which is transitional in character, red burnished ware still predominates. The painted pottery is red on cream; the patterns are mainly geometric and resemble textiles, but a number of pieces show a bold curvilinear ornament with fantastic motifs, that seem to owe their origin to the maeandroid patterns found on the Çatal Hüyük seals. The latter 'fantastic' style remains the less common one until Level II B (late II) when it proliferates to a remarkable extent. The geometric patterns predominate from V–II A. The painted and unpainted monochrome wares employ the

93 Stone slab with incised features from Hacılar VI

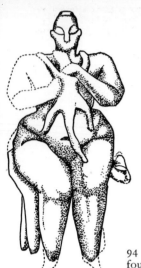
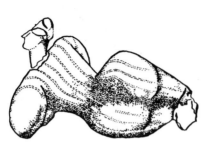

94 Group of naturalistic baked clay statuettes of the Mother Goddess found in houses in level VI (*cf. Ill. 89*) at Hacılar

same shapes, which are a development from those of Level IV, but collar-necked jars now appear as well as the oval Hacılar cup. Black monochrome ware or incised ornament do not occur at Hacılar, nor are there any cardial, nail-impressed or barbotine wares. The development of these fine painted wares appears to have occurred over a much more restricted area than the monochrome ware. Red pottery of Hacılar VI type covers a vast area from the Lake of Beyşehir to the Aegean coast, but the painted ware of Hacılar II–IV type is confined to the Burdur region. At Bucak south of Burdur a mound produced only the unpainted types, and none of the sites in the Maeander or Hermos valleys and their tributaries have yet produced painted pottery that looks earlier than Hacılar I (*c.* 5250–5000 BC). This may suggest that in the west of Anatolia monochrome ware lasted until the period of Hacılar I, when painted wares, perhaps of several versions, red on cream, white on red, etc., came into fashion.

This may have important bearings on the vexed question of Anatolian relations with Greece and the Balkans (see below p. 115).

Building remains of Levels V–III were not well preserved at Hacılar but they resemble the fortified enclosure

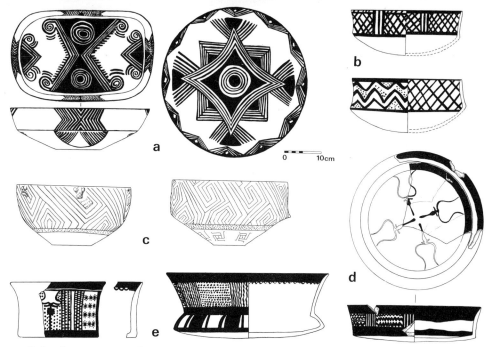

95 Painted pottery types from *a*, Hacılar; *b*, Çatal West; *c*, Can Hasan; *d–e*, Early Halaf

of Level II. Two methods of construction are found; building in mud-brick on stone foundations or houses built of wood with large posts and smaller ones in between, the whole covered by a thick plaster. Both methods had already been in use in Hacılar VI, but the post and plaster construction was only used there for kitchens. Figurines were only found in a fragmentary state, but they appear to be of the same types as we find in Level II. Most are red burnished, but some are painted and compared to Level VI the great variety of shapes has been reduced to four main types; standing, seated with the legs on one side, kneeling or resting. No single figure from our excavations was complete. The crude figurines with peg-heads, so common in Level VI, have disappeared. A head from Level V is unusual in that it has eyes in the form of a plastic pellet with a slit made by a nail impression. This is the common way of fashioning eyes of figurines in Greece, but unique in Anatolia.

Ill. 101

97, 98 Stone bowl and oval cup from Hacılar II

Hacılar II (c. 5435–5250 BC) marks the climax of this painted pottery culture and the fortified enclosure excavated is probably only part of the entire settlement. Within a thick mud-brick wall houses, a granary, potters' workshops and domestic courtyards are grouped around a number of large courts. Two phases of building, separated by a disastrous fire which laid the eastern half of the complex in ashes, can be distinguished architecturally and by the pottery. In the earlier phase a shrine with a deep well next door in an open yard was found in the north-east corner. In plan it resembled the large buildings of Level VI, and in the back wall it had two recesses in one of which the lower part of a stone slab was found. This again reminds one of the stone slabs of Level VI. Below the floor of this building three graves were found each containing a woman and child. Some painted pottery accompanied the dead. This is the only case in which burials were found inside a house, a number of others in Levels IV–VI lay below courtyard floors, with a red burnished bowl (IV), a marble cup and some

beads (V) and a pottery cup and bone pin (VI) as sole funerary gifts. All burials were contracted, but no fixed orientation could be observed. The quality of the pottery and figurines from Hacılar II is superb; the oval cups and bowls with fantastic design occur in large quantities and a special, and probably ritual, anthropomorphic vessel in the form of a goddess is frequently provided with eyes inlaid with obsidian. The figurines are larger than in the earlier levels, and though technically perfect, they lack the naturalistic grace of those from Level VI. Figures of the goddess with a child or with animals are no longer found and male statues have completely disappeared. Noteworthy is the reappearance of the stamp-seal with incised geometric design.

Ills. 95, 96, 100

Ill. 99

The settlement of Hacılar II perished in a conflagaration *c.* 5250 BC and thereafter some newcomers appear to have arrived with different traditions of building, pottery manufacture and figurines. They remodelled the site, using the old mound as a roughly circular court round which they threw huge blocks of rooms separated by courtyards and surrounded by a strong defensive wall. Of this fortress of Hacılar I a–b, only the basement plan survives but the plans of individual rooms with huge internal buttresses shows a continuity in architectural principles. The upper storey or storeys were of wood and some brick and when the fortress was destroyed by fire the contents of the upper storey collapsed with the burnt bodies of the defenders into the basement rooms, from which there was no escape. The newcomers of Level I probably came from neighbouring regions and they probably intermarried with the remains of the earlier population. Of their economy we know virtually nothing; no grain was found and few animal bones (mainly deer). Trade continued to import the necessary raw materials and there was no change in burial customs. Both in shape and decoration the pottery is markedly different and

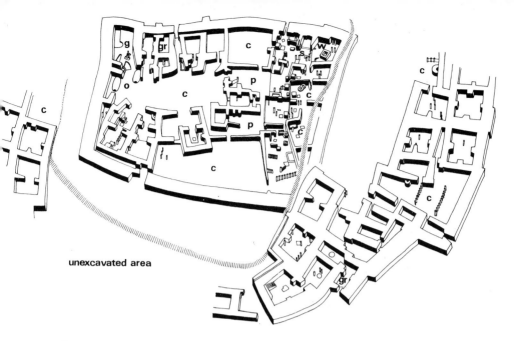

unexcavated area

101   Isometric view of fortified settlement of Hacılar II A, *c.* 5400 BC and the remains of the later fortress of Hacılar I, *c.* 5250 BC. *c*, courtyard; *g*, granary; *gr*, guardroom; *p*, potters' workshops; *w*, well; *s*, shrine

more than two thirds is now painted. Red and cream monochrome wares continue to be made, but most is painted in a linear style in red on white, with a small percentage in white on red. No single Level II shape survives except the 'toby-jug'. Ovals and ovoids, basket shapes, square and oblong vessels abound and the quality, though often excellent, rarely compares with that of Hacılar II. In the patterns a strong influence of basketry design is felt. In the figurines strong schematization sets in combined with incised ornament and a marked decrease in size. Traces of copper are found here as in the other levels of the site, but bone and stone tools continue the essentially neolithic tradition. The stamp-seals of Level II have disappeared and there are a few crude figurines of animals, which although so common at other sites, are almost absent at Hacılar. Two building-levels with squatters' remains overlay the burnt ruins of the fortress, and the site appears to have been deserted *c.* 5000 BC.

Ill. 100

113

Recent excavations in the Konya plain have shed some light on the cultures that followed the neolithic of Çatal Hüyük, but neither at Çatal Hüyük West (the site across the river) nor at Can Hasan, some fifty miles farther east, has a link been established with the neolithic.

Ill. 95

At the former site soundings established a succession of two different phases of painted pottery; an earlier painted in red on buff (Çatal Hüyük West ware) and a later and finer with paint in brown or black on a white slip (Can Hasan 2b ware). The excavations at Can Hasan show the same succession with the Çatal West ware in Level 3 and the painted white slip ware in Level 2b. With it appears a fine burnished ware, grey, buff or black, incised with maeandroid designs like those of the Çatal neolithic seals and rows of dots between lines with frequently below the rim a modelled bull's head. The same maeander-like patterns are found in wall-paintings fallen from an upper floor in a burnt settlement (Level 2b) that in plan shows remarkable resemblances to the fortress of Hacılar I. Large figurines of a distinctive type and copper objects (a mace-head and a bracelet) come from the same level, and imported pottery of Mersin XXI–XX type was found in the ruins. On the other hand sherds of the earlier Çatal West ware were found in Mersin XXIV–XXII so that evidence now exists for linking up developments on the plateau with those in the Cilician plain. Similarly after the destruction of Can Hasan 2b, new forms and styles of painted pottery appear in Level 2a which can be linked to Mersin XIX and XVIII, which also sees the first import of North Mesopotamian Halaf wares. Numerous carinated bowls with distinct designs from Çatal Hüyük West (period Can Hasan 2b) offer striking parallels to some Early Halaf vessels with which they may even be contemporary. Before we turn to a discussion of this interesting culture the relations between western Anatolia and the regions beyond the Aegean must be discussed.

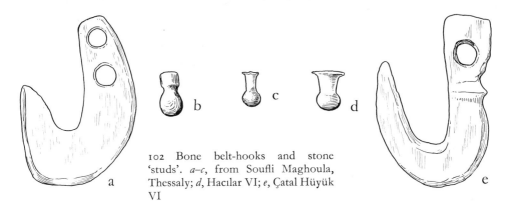

102 Bone belt-hooks and stone 'studs'. *a–c*, from Soufli Maghoula, Thessaly; *d*, Hacılar VI; *e*, Çatal Hüyük VI

Anatolia and South-eastern Europe

Even if we bear in mind the fact that no single group of people in the Near East ever completely copied the culture of its neighbour – in fact when they borrow they always introduce elements of their own – the similarity between the development of the earliest neolithic in Greece and western Anatolia is such that some obvious borrowing took place.

The quality of the earliest pottery so far found in Greece shows quite clearly that the first contacts with Anatolia were not established at the time when pottery was a primitive product at Çatal Hüyük (*c.* 6500–5900 BC), but came after. Even in Central Greece, which compared to the richer plains of Thessaly and Macedonia, may have been a little retarded and provincial, the earliest monochrome wares with which the sequence starts, have been dated by C-14 to *c.* 5520 BC and there seems little reason to push the first appearance of pottery in Greece back beyond 5600 BC when it first appeared in common use at Çatal Hüyük VI A *c.* 5900 and *c.* 5700 at Hacılar. The resemblance of the earliest Thessalian wares to the pottery of Çatal Hüyük or Kızılkaya is no indication of date, for exactly the same sort of pottery could be found at Çatal Hüyük as late as Level II (fifty-eighth century), or as early as Level VI A (fifty-ninth). An aceramic culture precedes the one with the earliest pottery in Thessaly and from one of its sites, Soufli Maghoula, come a number of so-called bone fish hooks and stone ear-studs (the latter

Ill. 102

115

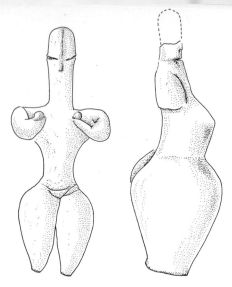

103 Two unbaked clay figurines from a shrine at the Early Neolithic site of Nea Nikomedeia in Greek Macedonia

also at Gremnos). Whereas such an 'ear-stud' came from Hacılar VI, destroyed *c*. 5600 BC, the 'fish hooks' are almost certainly belt-hooks, typical of Çatal VI A, dated to *c*. 5950–5880 BC. The aceramic of Thessaly can therefore probably be dated pre-5600 BC and the introduction of good pottery that follows it is probably related to the movement that carried Hacılar VI ware to the Aegean coast, to Chios and Skyros and beyond. The prolonged period of the use of monochrome pottery in Greece may possibly be paralleled in the coastal regions of western Anatolia until the appearance of painted wares (red on white, white on red) in Hacılar I (*c*. 5250–*c*. 5000) which accords well with a date of 5080 BC for the first appearance of red on white ware at Elateia in Central Greece (and 'Proto-Sesklo' in Thessaly). In Thessaly a phase with cardial and barbotine wares, evidently derived from Macedonia and the north intervenes between the Proto-Sesklo and the Middle Neolithic Sesklo culture (beginning *c*. 5000 BC). This native Balkan decoration, it should be emphasized, is not to be confused with that of Cilicia and the Levant, or that of Dalma in Azerbaijan. At Nea Nikomedeia in Macedonia large-scale excavations of an Early Neolithic settlement show eloquent evidence of Anatolian influence, and of local adaptation.

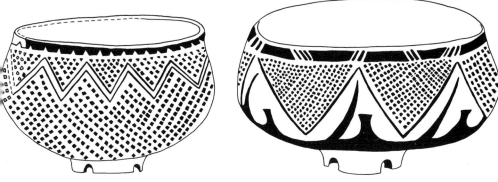

104 White and red painted pottery from the Middle Neolithic sites of Slatina and Kremikovci, Sofia region, Bulgaria. Late sixth millennium BC

In contrast to Anatolia, rectangular houses were free standing in an 'open settlement' pattern. They were of fairly large size, comparable to Hacılar VI, and consisted of a main room, a storeroom or kitchen and sometimes a porch, all built of wooden posts and plaster. A large building in which five Anatolian-looking clay statuettes were found was probably a village shrine. Most of the pottery is monochrome slipped and burnished ware, red, buff, greyish and with shapes reminiscent of Hacılar VI–V, but some is painted in red on white, and white on red and finger or nail impressed coarser ware also occurs. The association of these ceramic constituents is reminiscent of Proto-Sesklo and Pre-Sesklo (cardium, etc.) in Thessaly towards the end of the sixth millennium. Parts of 'toby-jugs', vessels made in the form of a goddess, also point to a comparatively advanced date (at Hacılar Levels II and I) and the 'stamp-seals' found are closest to those of Hacılar II. The dead were buried in a contracted position in the settlement, but without funerary gifts. Impressions on the bottoms of pots show twilled matting as at Hacılar and Çatal Hüyük and twining, also found in Çatal Hüyük VI fabrics. Weaving was therefore well advanced and spindle-whorls and loomweights have been found. The chipped stone industry is unspectacular, like that of

Ill. 103

Hacılar, and the material used is flint or chert, not obsidian. Serpentine axes, adzes and chisels, fully polished do not differ from their Anatolian counterparts. Belt hooks made of bone are quite common. Farming is the basic economy of this settlement; domesticated sheep and goats predominate, cattle and pig are less conspicuous. Wheat, barley, lentils, peas and acorns and pistachios have been found, but the exact varieties of wheat and barley are not yet known, and eagerly awaited.

Farther north and east, sites like Porodin and Vršnik appear to have yielded similar remains, especially the latter and C-14 dates of *c.* 5160 and 4915 (for a late phase, Starčevo III?) from these sites lend support to the archaeological equations. Both at Vršnik, and in the Sofia Basin and the Maritsa valley of Bulgaria the white-painted wares are common and characteristic of the Middle Neolithic, the Early Neolithic having only monochrome wares, plain or ornamented with barbotine, nail or finger imprints. Many of the painted pots are bowls on feet, a type characteristic of Hacılar II and the sickles, axes, etc., of the open settlement of Karanovo comparable to Nea Nikomedeia remind one unmistakably of similar material from Hacılar.

However, in the absence of excavated sites of this period in western or north-western Anatolia off the high plateau, it would be incautious to attempt to draw too close comparisons between Hacılar and sites in Greece, Macedonia and Bulgaria. Much that looks strange at the moment may have developed in the intermediate areas, untested by excavation and until we know what the equivalents of Hacılar were on the western seaboard of Anatolia it is impossible to say whether the related cultures across the Aegean or the sea of Marmora were the result of primary Anatolian colonization or secondary interaction of advanced Anatolian ideas and culture on a local and receptive European substratum.

Ill. 104

CHAPTER EIGHT

The Halaf and Later Cultures

The Halaf culture
(Late sixth and fifth millennium)

In contrast to most of the ceramic neolithic cultures so far described outside Anatolia, our information about the Halaf culture is comparatively full, even if no excessive amount of digging has produced this evidence. The type site is the village of Arpachiyah near Mosul for at the site of Tell Halaf, which gave its name to the culture, the pottery was found unstratified below later buildings. It would seem that metal was known, justifying the term 'Chalcolithic' used for this period.

The distribution of the Halaf culture describes an arc from the Euphrates to the Greater Zab. Whereas its southern limit is well defined, its northern is probably formed by the Taurus mountains, with pockets here and there on the plateau farther north.

The Halaf culture is a particularly vigorous one, owing nothing to Hassuna or Samarra. It was probably produced by newcomers from the north, and its original homeland probably lies in 'Turkish Mesopotamia'. At least two main variants can be distinguished in the pottery; an Eastern Halaf, best known from Arpachiyah and Tepe Gawra near Mosul, and a Western Halaf from sites such as Chagar Bazar, Tell Halaf and Yunus-Carchemish in Syria. Each of the two areas have local preferences for shape and decoration, which shows three phases of development and increasing elegance. The earliest with relative simple shapes among which the 'cream bowl' is already present prefers naturalistic ornament – bull's heads, heads of moufflon, or entire animals, leopards, deer, snakes, scorpions, birds, onagers as well as human beings and schematized trees, plants and flowers. Closely packed lines, straight or wavy, fields of dots and circles often placed in panels still remind one of the pattern burnished ware of the previous period, but they are the same simple ornament as is used in the decoration of copper vessels seen in Near Eastern bazaars today. The metallic shapes of much of the Halaf ware has not escaped observation and it is perfectly possible that early metal vessels contributed to the development of this remarkable civilization. Early metalworking in the region of Diyarbakir ('Copperland') near the centre of the Halaf homeland is indeed suggestive, and needs investigation. The early Halaf pottery is decorated in red or black on an apricot ground and highly polished. In the middle phase a cream slip is produced and more elaborate shapes are found with sharp flaring rims. Naturalistic ornament disappears except for the ubiquitous bucrania, which become more stylized Typical ornament consists of elaborate fields of geometric designs, which strongly resemble textile products, balanced by curving lines, scale patterns, dots, suns and stars. In the final phase great polychrome plates with elaborate centre-pieces such as rosettes and Maltese crosses, are produced in the east, to become one of the outstanding products of Near Eastern pottery.

Although the Halaf pottery is the most outstanding product of this civilization, there are numerous other aspects of great interest; architecture, religion, stone carving, weaving and trade.

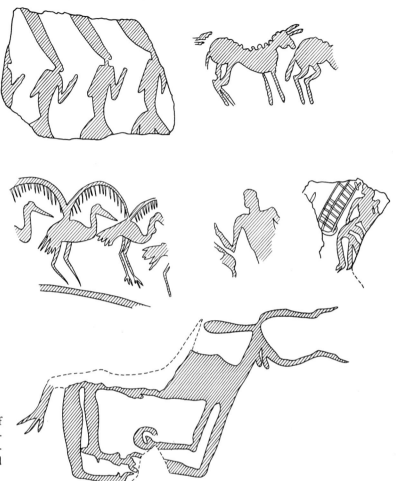

105 · Early Halaf pottery with naturalistic representations of people and animals

The peculiar architecture of the Halaf period is well known. The villages consisted of two-roomed houses set along paved roads. Each house consisted of a round domed inner room and a long rectangular ante-room, which may have had a gabled roof as is suggested by a stone pendant in the form of a wooden house. These buildings had stone foundations with a superstructure of mud-pads, as shaped mud-brick had not yet been invented in Mesopotamia. Bread ovens, hearths and bell-shaped storage pits were found in the settlement at Tell Turlu, west of the Euphrates, showing that here at least these structures were dwelling-houses and not shrines as was

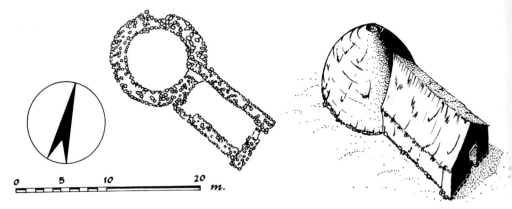

106 Reconstruction and plan of a 'tholos' at Arpachiyah. Halaf culture, Middle Chalcolithic period

Ill. 106

suggested for similar buildings at Arpachiyah. The largest there had walls 2 to 2.5 metres thick, a domed chamber 10 metres in diameter and an ante-room 19 metres in length. The Yunus domed rooms reach diameters of up to 6 metres. The only purely rectangular building at Arpachiyah was the potter's shop in the top level, but the remains of a shrine, containing the horn cores of a bull found at Tell Aswad on the River Balikh in Syria were of rectangular construction. No round buildings have been found either in Cilicia or in the Syrian province west of the Euphrates; rectangular architecture continued from the previous period. Contracted burials were found in the settlement at Arpachiyah, accompanied by rich gifts including clay figurines.

The Halaf people were farmers; flint sickle blades, glossy from reaping were found by the hundreds and models of sickles were made in soapstone. They grew emmer wheat and hulled two-row barley, with six-row barley making its first appearance towards the end of the period. Flax was grown for the extraction of linseed oil and perhaps for the production of linen.

The patterns on the pots testify to the high development of woven stuffs, perhaps still mainly in wool. Our

107 Polychrome plate typical of the end of the Halaf period in North Iraq from Arpachiyah

knowledge of animal husbandry is based more on figurines and pottery than on animal bones. Cattle, goat, sheep and a dog like a Saluki were probably domesticated, but there is proof only for the first two. The prominence of the bull in the cult does not by itself indicate domestication. On the contrary, the enormous horns of the bulls on the pottery suggest that it was the wild bull that was venerated as the emblem of male fertility. The occasional appearance of the ram in the same function is paralleled in the neolithic of Anatolia.

Hunting was evidently still practised; both arrowheads and slingstones are found. Fragments of hunting scenes show dogs on the leash or a bull caught in a trap. Hares, onagers, boars and numerous birds are shown on pots and they no doubt contributed to the larder. Many of the naturalistic paintings seem somewhat inappropriate on pottery and, on analogy with neolithic Anatolia, one is tempted to suggest that they may have been copied from wall-paintings, fragments of which have, however, yet to be found.

If the bucrania and the ram's heads point to a cult of the male fertility element, the frequent clay figures of women (and never of men) seated or squatting clearly demonstrate the cult of the Mother Goddess. As in Anatolia these figurines are frequently painted with lines and crosses (which is still the symbol of fertility in Anatolia). The execution of these statuettes is, however, schematic and primitive. Other cult symbols are the bull's hoof (or phallic?) pendants and the so-called double-axe, carved into beads (as in neolithic Anatolia) painted on pottery or woven into textiles.

Numerous other amulets show model sickles, winnowing-fans, ducks, and a house model, all carved in soft stone. Simple square or round seals are made of the same material and ornamented with simple incised designs. Models in stone of human finger bones are found, but the real masterpieces are the beads, plaques and vessels cut from obsidian. The use of native copper and lead is beyond doubt, but the metallic shapes of the pottery bear witness to more advanced techniques.

Trade was evidently well organized and extensive; obsidian from the Lake Van area and Indian Ocean shells obtained via the Persian Gulf found in the Halaf settlements are balanced by Halaf pottery at Tilkitepe near Lake Van (possibly a Halaf emporium) and elsewhere in the Malatya region, rich in copper and gold. Halaf imports and influence are seen in the bowl shapes, rosette patterns, bucrania and glaze paint which extends from the Persian Gulf to the Mediterranean. Trade was evidently carried on through intermediaries, but it must have been controlled by developed societies at home. Never before had one single culture dominated such a large expanse of territory.

The observant reader may have noticed a considerable number of resemblances and similarities between the Halaf culture of the late sixth and early fifth millennium (based on C-14 dates of 5288 for Arpachiyah TT8 and end of Amuq B at Ugarit, c. 5450 BC) and the Neolithic and Early Chalcolithic cultures of Anatolia. These were coming to an end and at just about the time that the Halaf culture first developed and from c. 5000 BC onwards the centre of cultural and technological development shifted first to north and after the fall of the Halaf culture, to southern Mesopotamia. It is tempting to regard this shift of the cultural centre of the Near East eastward not as a coincidence but as the result of the blotting out of the Hacılar and Çatal West cultures in the west. Without suggesting that refugees, or shall we say craftsmen, from the west found new patrons in the east – which may or may not have been the case – the 'Anatolianness' of much in the Halaf tradition can hardly be denied. The religion, including a bull cult, metalworking, weaving, the superb pottery and the higher technology in general cannot but remind one of Çatal Hüyük, Hacılar and Can Hasan already discussed above.

The end of the Halaf culture was brought about, it is thought, by invasion from the south of Mesopotamia. Extensive irrigation may have produced a surplus population in the 'Ubaid culture which set out to find new land. The Halaf culture was wiped out or disappeared, probably c. 4400–4300 BC, but not without leaving here and there pockets of at least cultural resistance.

The Transitional Period from Halaf to 'Ubaid along the Mediterranean Coast

As direct neighbours of the Western Halaf culture the region from Aleppo to Antioch came under strong Halaf influence, mixed in places with Samarra motifs. Imports and local imitation of Halaf schemes dominates the Amuq C culture and even Ras Shamra on the coast, where the local pattern burnished tradition. eventually died out. However, this region preserved its local characteristics, and in the following Amuq D culture representing the transitional period from Halaf to 'Ubaid this is very clearly shown. A local polychrome pottery appears with shapes that are partly derived from Halaf, partly from a new red-washed ware, which we shall soon encounter in its spread southwards to Palestine. Possibly it is representative of a new element, for wherever it appears it marks a break in the local tradition, and is associated with a general poverty in remains and architecture and accompanied by a new stone industry, best known from Byblos Late Neolithic and from Tell Ghassul in Jordan. The possibility that we are dealing here with semi-nomadic elements is strong; and the only buildings associated with this culture are flimsy structures at Byblos or subterranean round 'houses' in Palestine (Jericho Pottery Neolithic A–B complex, Tell esh Shuna ware in the Jordan valley and Wadi Rabah ware on the coast). In Palestine these northerners supplanted the Yarmukian culture, at Byblos the Middle Neolithic, and in the north they are associated with Late 'Halaf' painted pottery. Even in the south some painted styles, like those of Ghrubba (and Jericho IX or Pottery Neolithic A?)

occur with faint Syrian affiliations. At Byblos there is no trace of painted pottery. Characteristic of all these versions is the new stone industry and the red pottery with jars having loop handles or lugs, bases with mat imprints, rims leaning or curving inward (bow-rims), and carinated or hemispherical bowls. Bands of red paint alternate with plain red-washed surfaces. The general impoverishment in culture; the semi-nomadic aspect, the insubstantial remains create a vivid picture of the misery and disturbance that accompanied the break-up of the Halaf culture in the north. At Ras Shamra (IIIc) this new poverty-stricken phase is dated by C-14 to *c.* 4582 BC.

In the Lebanon and Palestine prosperity did not return until new elements arriving from the north *c.* 3600–3500 BC introduced the 'eneolithic' and Beersheba-Ghassulian cultures.

As usual, the rich lands of north Syria made a faster recovery. New elements from the south-east bringing with them an 'Ubaid tradition of painted pottery, established themselves from Hama on the Orontes to the Malatya region on the Anatolian Plateau. Some penetrated into the plain of Antioch where they produced the inartistic pottery of Amuq E. Elsewhere in the plain more gifted elements survived to fashion the Tell esh Sheikh ware, now also known from Ras Shamra, in which Halaf and 'Ubaid elements of deşign are combined into pleasing compositions, even if technically production was poor. At Ras Shamra old techniques died hard; polychromy survived and a new pottery combined Halaf and 'Ubaid motifs with pointillé incision in reserved fields. Seven successive building-levels are found at Ras Shamra during the 'Ubaid period and settled conditions if not prosperity had evidently returned by *c.* 4368 BC according to a C-14 date (first 'Ubaid Level III B).

Cilicia, sheltered from the Anatolian Plateau by the high ranges of the Taurus and from Syria by the wooded

Amanus, shows an even more complicated sequence of events. Halaf influence was here superimposed at Mersin XIX–XVII on a strong local painted pottery tradition, which had close links with the Konya Plain on the plateau of Anatolia. Halaf sherds reached the Konya Plain in small quantities, evidently as the result of trade, and in exchange we find polychrome ware at Mersin emanating from the Can Hasan 2a culture near Karaman, long before polychromy was practised in the Halaf culture. Anatolian influence steadily increased and by Mersin XVI an intrusive culture was well established in the famous fortress built, we may assume, against the easterners in the plain. Copper tools and weapons now first appear in quantity and the pottery has new shapes, wares and patterns which are Anatolian and have nothing to do with Halaf. Among the novelties the first use of handles on pots must be noticed. Just before its destruction, perhaps *c.* 4350 BC, the first 'Ubaid imports reached the fortress and after its destruction 'Ubaid influence gradually gained ground. It was, however, far from pure and the closest parallels point to the Tell esh Sheikh ware, whereas others show strong parallels with Ras Shamra III B, such as the incised and painted pottery of Level XV and the polychrome ware which continues in use. Mersin XV rebuilt as a fortress was destroyed and in XIV and XIII Anatolian burnished wares, mostly plain but some incised, appear side by side with the local 'Ubaid pottery. Finally a local painted ware at Tarsus and in the east of the plain shows lingering Halaf influence and a cemetery at the same site the influence of a new monochrome ware related to Amuq F, Hama and Byblos (*c.* 3500 BC). At Mersin on the other hand, renewed influence from the Konya Plain introduced a dark burnished ware, ornamented in white paint or, peculiar to Cilicia, with pattern burnish. Finally *c.* 3200 BC a further Anatolian wave introduced the Early Bronze Age.

These developments in Cilicia have been sketched here in some detail to illustrate the complicated pattern of cultures that frequently are found in areas exposed to several influences at once. The city of Tepe Gawra in north Iraq provides a parallel in the transition from Halaf to 'Ubaid, to which we must now return.

The 'Ubaid Period

With the spread of the 'Ubaid culture, originally at home in southern Iraq, over the whole of Mesopotamia *c.* 4400–4300 BC there begins a new era in which were laid the foundations of Sumerian civilization and from now onwards Mesopotamia becomes the centre of the civilized Near East. As a prelude to the Sumerian civilization of the Uruk period, its full story really belongs to a later period, and we shall therefore content ourselves with some more general points.

The 'Ubaid culture appears to have developed in the south of Mesopotamia out of its comparatively sophisticated predecessor known as Hajji Muhammad, which as we have seen was a culture probably of south Iranian origin influenced to some extent by that of Halaf. Spread throughout Lower Mesopotamia from Ras el Amiya near Kish to Eridu its existence, let alone its prosperity, is unthinkable without the extensive use of irrigation. As the culture developed and irrigation techniques improved the rich and fertile plain soon became overpopulated. The early 'Ubaid culture was in existence by *c.* 4325 BC according to a radiocarbon date from Warka and soon after settlers from the south moved up the Tigris and Euphrates in search of new land. In the long history of Mesopotamia they were the first to do so, and were to be followed by numerous others; previously cultural advances had come from the north and east. In the north the Halaf culture broke up, in places not without resistance – at Arpachiyah there was destruction and massacre – and all over the vast domains of the Halaf culture 'Ubaid wares are found, even north of the Taurus mountains, in the plains of Malatya, Elazig and Palu. To the north-west 'Ubaid influence penetrated as far west as Mersin in Cilicia, but there it stopped. South-westwards Hama on the Orontes marks the southern limit of 'Ubaid wares. In the north-east 'Ubaid wares crossed the passes to Azerbaijan where the Pisdeli ware found south and east of Lake Urmia may pass as a local 'Ubaid. To the east contact was maintained with Khuzistan and trade routes were opened with the east.

Never before had a single culture been able to influence such a vast area, if only superficially. The pottery distribution, in spite of minor variations, is fairly uniform. Though technically competent, it was still made by hand and its decoration, simple, sparse linear and monochrome designs is rarely beautiful and can hardly have caused aesthetic satisfaction to people who had been used to the glories of Halaf ware. Important advances are made in the north in metalwork, which now includes cast axes of copper. Gold also makes its first appearance, but only at the end of the period. In the south metal is still rare if not absent and it is hardly likely that it was superior armament which contributed to the success of the 'Ubaid people. As with so many early cultures it is probably trade which, more than anything else was responsible for the prosperity of the period and efficient agriculture for their numbers. That populous towns existed in Mesopotamia at this period is evident not only from the great buildings, but from the large cemeteries. The cemetery at Eridu contained more than a thousand graves. Little is known of the economy, but in art the goat and the ibex take the place of the cattle and sheep of the Halaf period. Extremely lively scenes of human beings surrounded by animals are found at Tepe Gawra carved on seals in the steatite, diorite, serpentine, carnelian, haematite and lapis lazuli imported from distant

108 Reconstruction of the 'Ubaid temple in level XIII at Tepe Gawra, Late Chalcolithic period

Badakhshan at the foot of the Pamirs. These little seals of the 'Ubaid period should be compared to the stiff geometric examples of the Halaf period showing the different spirit which inspired the new civilization. Every now and then remarkably naturalistic scenes occur on the pottery especially at Tepe Gawra, where Halaf survivals are still notable, and also elsewhere.

Nothing, however, more clearly demonstrates the change in culture than the monumental temples which were now built in the cities. Built of mud-brick, which makes its first appearance, and sometimes on stone foundations they dominated the cities from the top of ancient mounds. At Eridu they were set on mud-brick platforms the origin of the temple tower or *ziggurat*, made by filling in earlier buildings, and a flight of steps gave access to a door in the long side of the building. This consisted of a long central room, 10 metres or more in length, with a broad platform at one end and an offering table at the other. The main room was surrounded on both sides by smaller rooms from which ladders led to an upper storey and the roof. The central part of the building was probably higher than the double-storeyed side rooms and lit by triangular windows. The outside of the building was ornamented with elaborate projections and recesses which remained a characteristic of all later sacred buildings in Mesopotamia. House plans were essentially similar, lacking only the panelled walls and the paraphernalia implicit in the cult. A house at Tepe Gawra XVI had traces of wall-painting in red and black, and an entire quarter excavated in Level XII gives one a vivid picture of urban life. The most monumental series of temples arranged round three sides of a court at Tepe Gawra XIII illustrates even better than Eridu the tremendous advances made in this period. Without the Eridu sequence of sanctuaries from the Eridu to the 'Ubaid period, however, the south Mesopotamian origin of this architecture would not have been believed. A quarter of a century ago it was firmly believed that the people of Al 'Ubaid were primitive marsh-dwellers living in reed huts, hunting, fishing and practising sporadic agriculture like the Marsh Arabs of today.

Ill. 108

Epilogue

Much important evidence lies buried in museums or in the notebooks of unpublished excavations, and what has been brought together here is but a fraction of what eventually will be published. The nature of this book is then that of an interim report and many of the statements made here will eventually need revision. This is inevitable and in particular the chronology of these early periods is in a state of constant flux.

In the foregoing pages we have seen man emerge from cave and rock shelter and learn the rudiments of civilization: the preservation of food and its production during the long Proto-Neolithic period. All our evidence suggests that this was a long and slow process, about which we still have much to learn. Next, in the Aceramic Neolithic, we saw him emerge as a successful farmer, living in neatly constructed villages, tilling the soil and making vessels of stone, wood or baskets, in which to store, cook or eat his food. He did some trading with his neighbours to obtain raw materials for the manufacture of tools, weapons and luxury goods and practised certain fertility rites that required the manufacture of figurines of a goddess and of animals. At the village level of subsistence this may have been the rule but the town of Jericho (Pre-Pottery Neolithic A) with its huge stone-built tower and defences clearly shows that higher forms of social structure had already arisen if the need was there. Besides, simple village trading posts and market towns had already made their appearance.

This is even clearer in the next phase, when the making of pottery, the manufacture of copper and lead trinkets and elaborate woven fabrics are added to the technological repertoire. The city of Çatal Hüyük, contemporary with Jericho Pre-Pottery Neolithic B or with the villages of Jarmo and Mersin, produced a neolithic civilization worthy of a metropolis. It was followed by a number of high cultures with painted pottery (as at Hacılar, Can Hasan) and cult statues of a quality unsurpassed in the Near East, artistically well in advance of any contemporary culture in the so-called Fertile Crescent, and spreading its influence to the coast of the Aegean and well beyond. The precocity of Anatolia at this period is perhaps also reflected in the rise of the Halaf culture on the periphery of Anatolia, which exercised considerable influence on southern Mesopotamia and less directly on some of the Iranian painted pottery cultures.

During the fifth millennium B C invasions of culturally inferior northern neighbours extinguished the painted pottery cultures of southern Anatolia and at the same time the 'Ubaid culture of south Mesopotamia extended northwards, putting an end to Halaf. From then onwards the centre of civilization in the Near East shifted to Lower Mesopotamia and its influence is felt from Mersin in Cilicia to the Zagros Mountains and beyond. Local cultures managed to survive in Syria and Palestine, but their impact on Near Eastern civilization is not obvious and in Egypt the earliest neolithic hardly antedates the beginning of the 'Ubaid period and appears to be quite unrelated to developments farther east.

Finally as a result of the Uruk 'invasion' of Mesopotamia early in the fourth millennium B C, the basis is laid for the first rise of a literate civilization in Sumer. By establishing trade with Egypt via Syria and Lebanon, both countries with their unlimited wealth due to irrigation, cultural if not political unity and far flung trade, come to dominate the future developments of civilization in the Near East for the next three millennia.

Bibliography

List of Illustrations

Index

Bibliography

Advances have been such in the field covered by this book since the publication of *The Dawn of Civilization* in 1961 that only the most recently published items are listed below. For a fuller bibliography referring to the earlier publications the reader is referred to *The Dawn of Civilization*, p. 389, II, Roots in the Soil.

Abbreviations

Anat. Stud.   *Anatolian Studies*
IEJ   *Israel Exploration Journal*
ILN   *Illustrated London News*
PEQ   *Palestine Exploration Quarterly*
PPS   *Proceedings of the Prehistoric Society*

General

ANATI, E. *Palestine before the Hebrews.* London, 1963
ARKELL, A. J. Review of Predynastic development in the Nile valley. In *Current Anthropology*, 6, 1965 (forthcoming)
BRAIDWOOD, R. J. and HOWE, B. *Prehistoric investigations in Iraqi Kurdistan.* Chicago, 1960 (*Stud. in Anc. Or. Civ.* 31)
COLE, S. *The Neolithic Revolution.* 3rd ed. London, 1963
ESIN, U. and BENEDICT, P. Recent developments in the prehistory of Anatolia. In *Current Anthropology*, 4, 4, 1963
NAGEL, W. Zum neuen Bild des Vordynastisches Keramikum in Vorderasien. In *Berliner Jahrbuch fur Vor- und Fruhgeschichte*, 1961, 1; 1962, 2; 1963, 3
PARROT, A. *Archéologie Mésopotamienne.* II, Technique et problemes. Paris, 1953
PERROT, J. Palestine-Syria-Cilicia. In Braidwood and Willey eds. *Courses towards urban life.* Chicago, 1960
Radiocarbon, vol. V, 1963
ZERVOS, C. *Naissance de la civilisation en Grèce.* 2 vols. Paris, 1962

Excavations

BOSTANCI, E. Y. The Belbaşı industry. In *Belleten*, XXVI, no. 102, 1962
BRAIDWOOD, R. J. and BRAIDWOOD, L. J. *Excavations in the plain of Antioch.* I. Chicago, 1960, and reviewed by M. E. L. Mallowan in *Antiquity*, September, 1963
CAUVIN, J. Les industries lithiques du tell de Byblos (Liban). In *L'Anthropologie*, vol. 66, 5–6, 1962
CONTENSON, H. DE Poursuite des récherches dans le sondage à l'ouest du temple de Baal. In C. F. A. Schaeffer, *Ugaritica*, IV. Paris, 1962
— New correlations between Ras Shamra and Al 'Amuq. In *Basor*, no. 172, December, 1963
— Sondages à Tell Ramad en 1963. In *Annales Arch. de Syrie*, XIV, 1964
FRENCH, D. H. Excavations at Can Hasan. In *Anat. Stud.*, XII, 1962, and XIII, 1963
KENYON, K. M. Excavations at Jericho, 1957–8. In *PEQ*, July–December, 1960
KIRKBRIDE, D. A brief report on the pre-pottery flint cultures of Jericho. In *PEQ*, July–December, 1960
— Excavation of a neolithic village at Seyl Aqlat, Beidha, near Petra. In *PEQ*, July–December, 1960, and *ILN*, January 19th, 1963
LIERE, W. J. VAN and CONTENSON, H. DE A note on five early neolithic sites in inland Syria. In *Annales Arch. de Syrie*, vol. XIII, 1963
— Holocene environment and early settlement in the Levant. In *Annales Arch. de Syrie*, XIV, 1964

MASSON, V. M. The first farmers in Turkmenia. In *Antiquity*, September, 1961

MELLAART, J. Excavations at Hacılar, Fourth Preliminary report. In *Anat. Stud.*, XI, 1961

— Excavations at Çatal Hüyük. In *Anat. Stud.*, XII–XIV, 1962–4, and *ILN*, February, 1st, 8th, 15th, 22nd and May 9th, 1964

MORTENSEN, P. On the chronology of Early Farming communities in Northern Iraq. In *Sumer*, XVIII, 1962

PERROT, J. Excavations at Eynan, 1959 season. In *IEJ*, 10, i, 1961

RODDEN, R. J. Excavations at the Early Neolithic site at Nea Nikomedeia, Greek Macedonia (1961 season). In *PPS*, XXVIII, 1962, and *ILN*, April 11th and 18th, 1964

SOLECKI, R. S. Prehistory in Shanidar valley, North Iraq. In *Science*, vol. 139, no. 1551 (January 18th, 1963)

STEKELIS, M. and YIZRAELY, T. Excavations at Nahal Oren. Preliminary report. *IEJ*, 13, 1, 1963

STRONACH, D. B. The excavations at Ras Al Amiya. In *Iraq*, XXIII, 1961

THEOCHARIS, D. R. From the Pre-Pottery Neolithic in Thessaly. In *Thessalika*, 1, 1958. (In Greek, short English summary)

WEINBERG, S. S. Excavations at prehistoric Elateia. In *Hesperia*, XXXI

YOUNG, T. C. Jnr. Dalma Painted Ware. *Expedition*, Winter 1963

List of illustrations

The author and publishers are grateful to the many official bodies, institutions and individuals mentioned below for their assistance in supplying illustration material. Illustrations without acknowledgment are from original photographs by Mrs Mellaart.

139

54 Woman's grave with an obsidian mirror. Çatal Hüyük, level VI

55 Ceremonial pressure-flaked flint dagger from a male burial. Çatal Hüyük, level VI

56 Necklace from Çatal Hüyük, level V

57 Textile fragment (wool ?) from a burial. Çatal Hüyük, level VI

58, 59 Black burnished pottery. Çatal Hüyük, level VI A, c. 5900 B C

60 Basket burial. Çatal Hüyük, room E VI, B.20

61 Group of contracted burials below the platforms of a shrine. Çatal Hüyük, level A VI, 1

62 Reconstruction of a shrine with wall-paintings of vultures pecking at human bodies. Çatal Hüyük, shrine E VII, 8. Drawn by Grace Huxtable

63 Wooden box with lid from a burial. Çatal Hüyük, level VI

64 Baked clay seal with intricate designs. Çatal Hüyük, level IV

65 Shrine painting with two vultures with human legs attacking a headless human body. Çatal Hüyük, shrine E VII, 21. c. 6150 BC

66 Bead necklaces, bracelets and bone belt-hooks. Çatal Hüyük level VI

67 Female burial with red painted skull. Çatal Hüyük, room E VI, B.20. c. 6000 B C

68 Plan of building-level VI B, Çatal Hüyük, c. 6000 BC. Drawn by Gerard Bakker

69 Wooden vessels of fir tree wood. Çatal Hüyük level VI. Drawn by Grace Huxtable

70 Brown limestone boy-god on leopard, height 5.5 cm. Çatal Hüyük, shrine E VI, 10

71 Blue limestone standing goddess and leopard, height 11 cm. Çatal Hüyük, shrine E VI, 10

72 Limestone concretion with sculptured head, height 19.6 cm. Çatal Hüyük, shrine E VI, 10

73 Baked clay figure of a seated goddess, height 16.5 cm. (excluding head). Çatal Hüyük, shrine A II, 1

74 White marble figure of an old goddess, height 17 cm. Çatal Hüyük, shrine E VI, 25

75 White marble figure of a vulture (?), length 6 cm. Çatal Hüyük, shrine E VI, 25

76 Stone plaque with four human figures, height 11.5 c.m. Çatal Hüyük, house E VI, 30

77 White marble seated male figure, height, 12 cm. Çatal Hüyük, shrine level VI, 10

78 Alabaster bearded god seated on a bull, height 11 cm. Çatal Hüyük, shrine level VI, 44

79 White marble figure of a seated young god, height 21.5 cm. Çatal Hüyük, shrine E VI, 25

80 Reconstruction of the second phase of First Shrine, Çatal Hüyük, shrine E VI, 8. Drawn by Grace Huxtable

81 Painted relief of two leopards. Çatal Hüyük, shrine E VI, 44. c. 6000 B C

82 Reconstruction painting of a dead man's head. Çatal Hüyük, shrine in level IV, c. 5825 B C

83 Pregnant goddess in moulded relief. Çatal Hüyük, shrine E VII, 23. c. 6150 BC

Index

Numbers in italics refer to illustrations